SELF-DISCIPLINE

Overcome Procrastination, Manage Your Anger, Improve Your Relationships, Develop Self-Control and Mental Toughness

Sarah Miller

© Copyright 2020 by Sarah Miller. All right reserved.

The work contained herein has been produced with the intent to provide relevant knowledge and information on the topic on the topic described in the title for entertainment purposes only. While the author has gone to every extent to furnish up to date and true information, no claims can be made as to its accuracy or validity as the author has made no claims to be an expert on this topic. Notwithstanding, the reader is asked to do their own research and consult any subject matter experts they deem necessary to ensure the quality and accuracy of the material presented herein.

This statement is legally binding as deemed by the Committee of Publishers Association and the American Bar Association for the territory of the United States. Other jurisdictions may apply their own legal statutes. Any reproduction, transmission or copying of this material contained in this work without the express written consent of the copyright holder shall be deemed as a copyright violation as per the current legislation in force on the date of publishing and subsequent time thereafter. All additional works derived from this material may be claimed by the holder of this copyright.

The data, depictions, events, descriptions and all other information forthwith are considered to be true, fair and accurate unless the work is expressly described as a work of fiction. Regardless of the nature of this work, the Publisher is exempt from any responsibility of actions taken by the reader in conjunction with this work. The Publisher acknowledges that the reader acts of their own accord and releases the author and Publisher of any responsibility for the observance of tips, advice, counsel, strategies and techniques that may be offered in this volume.

TABLE OF CONTENTS

Introduction 1
Chapter 1 *Introduction To Self-Discipline* 5
Chapter 2 *Willpower* 11
Chapter 3 *Motivation* 21
Chapter 4 *Goal Setting* 24
Chapter 5 *Procrastination* 32
Chapter 6 *Building Good Habits* 43
Chapter 7 *Increasing Your Self-Discipline* 55
Conclusion 66
Description 68

INTRODUCTION

Self-discipline is one of the most useful skills a person can have. It is a skill that people use in every area of life. Although many people understand the importance of this skill, not many take the time and effort to improve their discipline. A common myth for self-discipline is that those who practice it are always living in a strict and limited lifestyle. On the contrary, self-discipline merely means having better self-control and increasing one's inner strength to control themselves, their behavior, and reactions.

You're probably wondering, "What can I achieve through strengthening self-discipline?" You can achieve most of the goals you set for yourself as long as your mindset is there. Throughout this book, we will be learning about different ways that you can achieve self-discipline through. Popular techniques include visualization and meditation. These are techniques that people use to envision themselves, achieving the goals and success that they want in life. By picturing what they want, people have achieved goals that they never thought were possible by merely altering their mindset and overcoming bad habits. People such as athletes and entrepreneurs all rely heavily on their self-discipline ability to achieve the success that they want. Those in industries where their success highly depends on their ability to perform tend to showcase better self-discipline behavior due to having more practice from exercising it every day. For example, people in sales tend to showcase more self-discipline than other occupations because of the targets that they have to meet. People within the sales industry usually are hired due to their motivation to make money. By having a defined goal, they feel motivated to do everything they can to reach it and are continuously overcoming obstacles like instant gratification and laziness. If a person is always overcoming those obstacles every day, those obstacles slowly start to feel like they aren't there anymore. That's when self-discipline becomes a habit. This habit is the goal that I want you to focus on as you read through this book.

One of the main traits of self-discipline is denying instant gratification and pleasure in return for a more significant gain, which requires a person to put in effort and time to achieve. Most people know that self-discipline is one of the most crucial components when it comes to success. Here is how self-discipline expresses itself:
- Self-control
- Perseverance
- The ability to not give up even when faced with obstacles and failure
- The ability to resist temptations or distractions
- The ability to keep trying until you accomplish the goal you've set

Self-control and willpower play a large role in one's self-discipline. Although both of these sound similar, self-control and willpower are slightly different from each other. A ton of research is being done in recent years to explain the numerous elements of willpower. Many professionals that study this area of self-control to this with one goal on their mind. They are about these types of questions: If willpower is a limited resource, what can we do to conserve it? How can we strengthen willpower?

A technique called "implementation intention" is another helpful tactic that helps improve willpower. These intentions are usually in the form of "if-then" statements that aid people in planning for situations that are likely to disrupt their goals. For instance, a person monitoring their sugar consumption may tell themselves before entering a dinner gathering that when the dessert comes out, they will refrain from eating it by instead eating fruit. Research has found that implementing solutions will increase self-control amongst adults and adolescents, even if people already had their willpower depleted by other tasks. People who have a plan ahead of time allow them to quickly make decisions without drawing upon their bank of willpower resources.

This research suggests that people who have a bank of willpower that is limited raises a few troubling questions. Are people destined to fail if they face too many temptations? The answer is not necessarily. Many psychologists have the belief that a person cannot ever completely use up their willpower. Instead, people often have stored some backup willpower for future demands. Those reserves are only available for the right type of motivation, allowing them to accomplish things even when their willpower has seemingly run out.

To demonstrate this idea, a researcher found out that individuals who had their willpower used up 'completely' continued to accomplish self-control tasks when they heard that they would be well-compensated for their actions. The same was true if they heard that their efforts would bring benefits to other people. He concluded that having high motivation can overcome weak self-control.

Willpower can also be manipulated in the first place to be less likely to become completely depleted. Psychologists often use an analogy to describe will power as being similar to a muscle that will tire out after many exercises. However, there is another element to this analogy. Although muscles will tire due to exercise during the short-term, they become stronger when regularly exercised over the long term. Just like physical exercise, self-control can become stronger when a person exercises willpower.

According to one of the earlier experiments that supports the idea above, the researchers asked participants in the study to follow a two-week guide to improve their moods, track their food intake, or enhance their physical posture. Compared to the group that didn't need to exercise self-control, the participants who had to use their willpower by performing willpower-heavy exercises were not as vulnerable to the depletion of self-control in a follow-up study. In another study, a scientist found that smokers who exercised willpower for two weeks by avoiding sweets or regularly squeezing an exercise handgrip found more success when it came to smoking cessation than other participants who performed two weeks of tasks that didn't require any self-control.

Other researchers have also discovered that using your willpower muscles can help a person increase the strength of their self-control over some time. Some researchers in Australia did a study where they assigned participants to a physical exercise program that lasted two months; this is a willpower-required routine. In the conclusion of this program, the participants who finished it scored better when measuring self-control than the other participants who were not assigned the exercise program. The participants that did the program also reported having been smoking less, eating healthier food, drinking less alcohol, improving their study habits, and monitoring their spending habits more carefully. Regular exercise of a person's willpower using physical exercise seems to have led to an increase of will power in their daily lives.

The research findings regarding how glucose levels tie into willpower depletion suggest a potential solution. A person who maintains their blood sugar by eating regularly and more often may have an easier time replenishing their willpower storage as their brain has energy. Those who are dieting aim to preserve their willpower to keep their diet going, but the calorie reduction may make this problematic. As a result, it may be more effective to eat frequent and small meals instead of skipping out on entire meals like lunch or dinner.

Studies also found that people who consume healthier foods were less likely to face this problem. This result came because of the amount of glucose people consumed.

High fructose corn syrup is undoubtedly an ingredient you have heard of before or at least one you have seen on the packaging of your favorite snacks or fast foods. While this does come from real corn, after it is fully processed, there is nothing corn-like about it. High fructose corn syrup is essentially the same thing as refined sugar when all is said and done. Companies use it as a sweetener in foods like soda, cereal, and other sweet and quick foods. Food production companies use this ingredient often because it is much cheaper than using sugar and is much easier to work with. High Fructose Corn Syrup is a common food additive that is very similar to sugar or glucose. This product is highly addictive. This substance is similar to cocaine in its addictive properties.

Eating certain foods makes the body feel rewarded, positive, and happy after they ingest them. These foods include convenience foods such as processed sugars or salts, fast food, and quick pastries. While these are the easiest to turn to, they can reduce a person's willpower resources, as we have seen through numerous studies.

All this evidence, founded from studies of the depletion of willpower, proposes that people making resolutions for the new year is the worst approach possible. If a person is running low on willpower in one specific area, it often reduces their willpower in all other areas. Focusing on one goal at a time makes more sense. In other words, don't try to get into a healthy diet right away, quit smoking, and start a new workout plan all at the same time. A much better technique is to complete goals one by one. Once you have one single good habit nailed, people no longer need to use their supply of willpower to maintain that behavior. Healthy habits will eventually become a part of a person's daily routine and would not need to use decision-making energy at all. There are still many questions regarding the nature of willpower that needs to be answered by future research. However, it seems like if somebody has clear goals, good self-monitoring, and does a little bit of practice, they can train their self-control to be strong when faced with temptation.

No matter how young or old, how inexperienced or experienced, or what education level you have, this book will help you strengthen your self-discipline so you can utilize it in your daily life to achieve the things you want to achieve. The things you want to achieve don't have to be huge goals like building your own billion-dollar company, but you can use it to start achieving some little things that you want in life. These little things could include; quitting smoking, eating healthier, or completing a personal project that's important to you. Regardless of who you are and what you want to accomplish, the basis of self-discipline is the same for everyone. This book will help you understand everything you need to know about self-discipline, the benefits and challenges it brings. It will provide you with a step-by-step process of achieving self-discipline and some practical exercises that you can use to strengthen it.

CHAPTER 1
Introduction To Self-Discipline

Before we touch on more detailed self-discipline topics, we must understand the benefits that it will bring into your life. Furthermore, understanding the most common causes of low self-discipline can help you identify the cause of this bad habit in your life. In this chapter, you will learn about the benefits that having strong self-discipline can bring. We will be discussing five main benefits that self-discipline can add to your life. Also, we will learn about what causes someone to have low self-discipline.

How Will Self-Discipline Benefit Your Life?

When a person has strong self-discipline, it leads to higher self-regard, inner strength, self-assurance, and satisfaction and happiness. It leads to better outcomes in every area of a person's life. The following benefits of self-discipline are ones that may not automatically come to mind.

1. Self-Discipline Increases Your Character and Mental-Strength

According to a famous psychology book, there was an important statement that the author wrote. He stated that everyone is the person that they wish to be. All that is stopping you from behaving in the manner you want to behave is your emotional mind. Let's think about that for a second. Although you may be a very kind and caring person, other people may see you as a hothead or an angry person if you tend to lose your temper easily. In this example, you don't necessarily need to change who you are as a person. Instead, you need to change the way you behave. Once you change the way you behave, other people will then see you for the person you truly are. For example, you are already a kind and caring person, but your short temper prevents you from showing that personality to the world. Self-discipline is a tool that can help you to stop acting on your impulses and instead act based on your true character.

2. Self-Discipline Improves Your Ability To Resist Temptations

Our modern-day lives are full to the brim with temptations that can throw people off track and prevent them from achieving their goals. Often, these temptations are temporary, and by exercising willpower, most people can overcome the urge. In our modern workplace, temptations tend to take the form of distractions like checking your phone, a conversation at the water cooler, or scrolling through social media. Those examples are just the tip of the iceberg when it comes to our potential modern-day distractions. When you can recognize your temptations, you can put a strategy in place to prevent caving to it. This method requires less self-discipline compared to ignoring the temptation with brute mental force. For example, your coworker locks her phone in her desk drawer and refuses to check her phone during the workday. She may make this strategy easier for her by telling her friends that she does this not to expect an immediate response.

Temptations also exist in the form of addictions and bad habits. When self-disciplined comes together with effective strategies, it is a very valuable tool that we can use to overcome most urges in life.

3. Self-Discipline Drives Success

When you can achieve a goal with great ease, some would argue that it should not be considered a goal. This opinion exists because goals require a person to stretch and grow; to improve skills, attitudes, and improve one's knowledge. When an individual meets those requirements, they improve their quality of life and improve their capability to take on larger and harder challenges. Ultimately, goals should be challenging. Everyone will face barriers and obstacles in which they would need to overcome. This action is needed to create personal growth that will help you overcome these obstacles and barriers to achieve your goals. It will require a lot of self-discipline and self-belief. A person's ability to persevere and overcome obstacles when faced with difficulty is often the difference between failure and success.

4. Self-Discipline Helps Improve Relationships

Take a minute to think about some of the things that you value in a relationship. The types of relationships could include a friendship, a romantic relationship, or a familial relationship. You may value important things like integrity, dependability, loyalty, and honesty. All of these traits require a person to have a strong character. It requires someone who can be true and act true to their values and beliefs, even when it would be easier to fall into temptation. As we already discussed, those with self-discipline are more likely to develop a stronger character. They have a lot of practice doing the things they know need to be done, even though they would probably rather be doing something else. Generally, they are a person on whom most people can count. They are more effective when it comes to gaining respect and building trust amongst their peers.

5. Self-Discipline Gives You Thicker Skin

People with more self-discipline tend to be calmer, assured, and more confident. They know who they are as a person and what their beliefs are. They will always do what they believe to be the right thing. As I have mentioned throughout this book, although the task that you need to do may not be something that you want to do at that very moment in time, the strength of self-discipline demands you to be true to your values and beliefs. One of the major benefits of this behavior of a self-disciplined person is that they can always be confident that they have done their best. If a person knows that they tried their very best and couldn't have done any better, they will be able to hold their heads up high, knowing that any insults or criticism are meaningless. However, this person would also be prepared to listen to any constructive criticism, but negative feedback does not affect them much. To maximize the benefits of self-discipline, a person must have goals that effectively motivate and inspire them.

The Most Common Causes of Low Self-Discipline

At this point, we've learned that having high self-discipline helps people establish their inner strength and character, enables them to withstand temptation, increases their chance of success, builds better relationships, and has more resistance to feeling offended. We will now discuss some of the causes as to why some people have low self-discipline. Having low self-discipline, not unlike high self-discipline, affects people's performance in multiple aspects of their lives. These aspects of life include; the performance at work, school, relationships, sports, and financial well-being.

Lack of self-discipline shows up in all the different things that people do in their lives. Some people make sure that they do the big things in life but neglect the little things. They do this to impress other people who don't know them very well. However, they tend to annoy and disappoint those close to them because it shows that they don't care enough about the people they should be showing respect. When people choose not to perform certain chores or duties, don't do what they say they would, don't show up for appointments, or don't make themselves presentable for every day, they show low self-discipline. So you may be wondering, why don't we take more responsibility for these everyday obligations? Below are two reasons why:

One of the reasons people don't take more responsibility for everyday obligations is because they don't believe in its importance. Why is this? Why do some people take the time to be considerate, clean, trustworthy, and honest While others believe that those things are important? The answer is their attitude towards themselves, other people, and life itself. The former believe that people, including themselves, and other life forms, are worth investing their energy, time, resources, and interest. They can see the importance of life while the latter have less regard for life and themselves. All of the simply relates to love. When people have a love for life, they tend to respect all components of it. They take the time to appreciate and experience life as if it's a pleasure. Self-discipline comes from the willingness to take care of ourselves, other people, and other types of life. The lack of discipline shows less willingness to respect themselves or other things.

The second reason people don't take more responsibility for everyday obligations is their lack of commitment. A person's commitment, enthusiasm, and interest in a task determine the degree to which they can be distracted. When their commitment is very high, very few things have the power to distract them, but if they are doing something meaningless to them, their attention is easily distracted. This evidence proves a strong link between self-discipline and commitment. People who cannot ignore, control, or bypass thoughts means that they have low self-discipline.

By learning why a person does not take more responsibility for everyday obligations, we are ready to learn the eight causes of poor self-discipline.

1. Low Self-Discipline Is Caused By The Lack Of Awareness

The primary cause of low self-discipline is a lack of awareness. This component is important specifically to our imagination and thinking. People are unaware that the thoughts that take our attention are negative and can damage a person's well-being. These thoughts are fed into the conscious mind by the negative mind power to ensure that people have minimal time to be mindful simply. If people are aware of the things that are happening within their minds, they would know that self-discipline is needed to refocus our attention away from the flow of negative thoughts.

2. Low Self-Discipline Can Be Due To Character Weaknesses

Often, people who have weak character also have poor self-discipline. Weak character includes the following; a low level of inner strength, mental toughness, courage, lack of love for other people, an absence of self-love, low interest in self-improvement, apathy, and a version of hard work, shortage of responsibility, lack of self-reflect, high levels of greed, and the inability to ignore Temptations in general.

If people place more importance on the desires, thoughts, and emotions that harm them more than the actions, thoughts, and people that help them, it will be difficult for them to develop high self-discipline. Each moment comes with a choice that a person has to make. They can either do something that helps them reach the goals that they have set for themselves, or they can fall into temptation and choose the action that has instant gratification.

3. Low Self-Discipline Can Be A Product Of Low Ambition

Ambition is very effective in creating self-discipline by motivating us to work towards our goals, although we might rather be doing something else. However, it harms our self-discipline if our ambition is an honorable, ethical, or fulfilling one. It is obvious that people who lack the ambition to achieve goals in life will have a harder time building strong self-discipline because they don't have a reason to do it. This reason is why we discussed in chapter one that one of the main steps in developing strong self-discipline is setting clear and attainable goals. By coming up with a realistic goal, an individual can then create a plan of action to hold themselves accountable. They also need to continue finding the motivation and ambition to keep them striving towards their goals.

4. Low Self-Discipline Can Be Caused By Having Unimportant Goals

People who have goals that aren't that important tend to lack the ambition to achieve them and, therefore, will not practice their self-discipline. Suppose people set goals that look good on paper but don't believe that they are necessary, or don't see them as goals that are important enough to accomplish in the first place. In that case, they may find it very difficult to exercise self-discipline and put in the work to achieve these goals. One of the main motivating factors of self-discipline is having a goal to stand by or is important to them. By having an important goal, or something meaningful to them, they will find the self-discipline needed to complete the tasks required to achieve their goal.

5. Laziness Can Cause Low Self-Discipline

There are many temporary reasons why a person is not exhibiting self-discipline to do what they need to do. These temporary reasons could be sickness, tiredness, apathy, or something more appealing than the task. If you find that these excuses were often occurring when you were trying to complete the task needed to reach a goal, you need to dig deep and find the real reason you choose options that aren't the ones that will help you achieve your goal. Laziness is often the culprit in a lot of cases. The reasons for laziness usually runs very deep into an individual's psyche. If a person believes that there is a worthwhile goal, they will be motivated to keep working and applying themselves and making the decisions that make sense when it comes to achieving their goal. However, suppose they don't have any motivation to achieve their goal. In that case, it likely means that their goal isn't important enough, or the person has a natural tendency to be lazy and uninterested.

6. Low Self-Respect Can Lower Self-Discipline

Often, a person who lacks self-respect doesn't put a lot of effort or importance in achieving personal excellence. They often don't care what others think about them or whether or not they are helping out other people in their lives. You might be wondering what self-respect has to do with self-discipline. The answer is that it takes self-discipline to produce excellent results, achieve goals, and help people who require it. When a person doesn't think about their self-improvement, they tend to focus on other things that please them, such as instant gratification. They don't necessarily practice self-discipline because they are comfortable in indulging the instant gratification that life throws at them. If a person lacks respect for themselves, they are more likely to indulge in unhealthy conveniences like fast food or shopping impulses discussed in chapter one. If a person does have self-respect for themselves, they understand that this instant gratification may bring them joy and pleasure at the moment, but does very little in helping them achieve healthy long-term goals.

By the end of this chapter, you have learned the benefits of having high self-discipline, the causes of low self-discipline, and its effects on a person when they have low self-discipline. By understanding the psychology behind the concept of self-discipline, willpower, and self-control, a person is more likely to see the importance of having these traits if they are a person that wants to achieve the goals they have in life. I strongly believe that everyone has their own goals that they want to accomplish in their life. Those who say they don't have goals may simply be too afraid. They may be afraid of failure and, thus, hide their fear behind their lies about how they don't have goals. They may do this instead of coming to terms with the fact that they are scared of failing to achieve their goals.

CHAPTER 2
Willpower

A common belief in people is that they think they can change their lives for the better if they simply could have more willpower. If people had more willpower, everyone would save responsibly for retirement, exercise regularly, stop procrastinating, avoid alcohol and drugs, and achieve all kinds of their noble goals. Understanding what the psychology behind self-discipline is extremely crucial will help you learn what the driving factors are behind it. One of the main factors that drive self-discipline is willpower. A survey that studied all Americans and their annual stress found that most participants reported that lacking willpower is the number one reason for not following the changes they want for themselves.

What Is Willpower?

In the survey that we just mentioned, results showed that the biggest obstacle to people achieving change was the lack of willpower. Even though many people often blame the scarcity of their willpower for their unhealthy choices, they are still grasping on to the hope of achieving it one day. Most people in this study also reported that they think willpower can be taught and learned. They are correct. Some research has recently discovered many ways in which people can strengthen willpower with training and practice.

On the contrary, some survey participants expressed that they think they would have more willpower if they had more free time to spare. However, their willpower is not something that increases automatically if a person has more time in their day. That leads me to the next question: How can people resist when they face temptation? Over the last several years, we have made many discoveries about how willpower works by scientists worldwide. We will dive a little deeper into what our current understanding of willpower is.

Weak willpower isn't the only reason for a person to fail at achieving their goals. Psychologists in the field of willpower have built three crucial components when it comes to achieving goals. They said that you first need to set a clear goal and then establish the motivation for change. They said the second component was to monitor your behavior in regards to that goal. Willpower itself is the third and final component. If your goal is similar to the following; stop smoking, get fit, study more, or stop wasting time on the internet, willpower is an important concept to understand if you are looking to achieve any of those goals.

The bottom line of willpower is achieving long-term goals by resisting temporary temptations and urges. Here are several reasons why this is beneficial. Over a regular school year, psychologists performed a study that examined self-control in a class of eighth-grade students. The researchers in this study did an initial assessment of the students' self-discipline by getting them, their parents, and teachers to fill out a questionnaire. They took it one step further and gave these students the task of deciding whether they want to receive $1 right away or $2 if they waited a week. At the end of the study, the results pointed out that the students who had better test scores, better school attendance, better grades, and had a higher chance of being admitted to competitive high school programs all ranked high on the self-discipline assessment. These researchers found that self-discipline played a bigger role than IQ when it came to predicting academic success. Other studies have found similar evidence. In a different study, researchers asked a group of undergraduate university students to fill out self-discipline questionnaires that researchers used to assess their self-control. These researchers developed a scale that helped score the student's concerning the strength of their willpower. They found that the students with higher self-esteem, better relationship skills, higher GPA, and had less alcohol or drug abuse all had the highest self-control scores from the questionnaire.

Another study found that the benefits of willpower tend to be relevant well past university years. Researchers conducted this self-control study on a group of 1000 people who they tracked since birth to the age of 32. This study is a long term study in New Zealand, where they wanted to learn more about the effects of self-control well into adulthood. They found that the people who had high self-control during their childhood grew up into adults with better mental and physical health. They also had fewer substance abuse problems, criminal convictions, better financial security, and better money-saving habits. These patterns were proven even after the researchers had adjusted external influences such as socioeconomic factors, general intelligence, and these people's home lives. These findings prove why willpower is extremely important in almost all areas of a person's life.

Now that you have learned the importance of willpower and its role in multiple stages of a person's life, let's define it a little further. We use many other names for willpower interchangeably; this includes; drive, determination, self-control, resolve, and self-discipline. Some psychologists will characterize willpower in even more specific ways. Some define willpower to be:

• The capacity to overcome unwanted impulses, feelings, or thoughts.
• The ability to resist temporary urges, temptation and delay instant gratification to achieve goals that are more long-term
• The conscious regulation of oneself.
• The ability to engage a "cool" cognitive system of behavior rather than a "hot" emotional system

- A limited resource that can be depleted

What Is the Importance of Willpower?

Over 40 years ago, a famous psychologist studied self-control within children using a simple and effective test. You may have seen this study used before in modern-day experiments. His experiment is called the "marshmallow test." This test has become extremely famous over the years as it laid the groundwork and then paved the way for modern studies of self-control.

This psychologist and his colleagues began the test by showing a marshmallow plate to a child at the preschool age. Then, the psychologist let the child know that he had to go outside for a few moments and let the child make a very simple decision. If the child could wait until the psychologist came back into the room, she could have two marshmallows. If the child could not or doesn't want to wait, she can ring the bell, which then the psychologist would come back to the room right away, but then she would only get to have one marshmallow.

We define willpower as simple as the ability for a person to delay instant gratification. Children who have high self-control can give up the immediate gratification of eating a marshmallow so that they can eat two of them later. People who have quit smoking sacrifice one cigarette's satisfaction to have better health and lower their risk of developing cancer in the future. Shoppers fight the urge to spend money at a mall to save their money for their future retirement. You probably get the point here.

This marshmallow experiment helped the researchers develop a framework that explains people's ability to resist or delay instant gratification. He proposed a system that he calls "hot and cool" to explain whether willpower will succeed or fail. The 'cool' system is naturally a cognitive one. It means that it is a thinking system that uses knowledge about feelings, sensations, goals, and actions that remind oneself of why the marshmallow shouldn't be eaten. The cool system is very reflective, while the hot system is more emotional and impulsive. The hot system is responsible for quick and reflex-based responses to specific triggers, for example, eating a single marshmallow without thinking about the long term ramifications. To put this in layman's terms, if this framework were a cartoon, the hot system would be the devil, and the cool system would be the angel on your shoulder.

When somebody's willpower fails, their hot system essentially overrides their cool system, which leads them to make impulsive actions. However, some people are more or less affected by the hot system triggers. That susceptibility to emotional responses plays a big role in influencing a person's behavior throughout life. The same researcher discovered that when he revisited his experiment with the same children who had grown into adolescents, he found that the teenagers who could wait longer (to have two marshmallows) when they were children were more likely to have higher SAT scores. Further, their parents were more likely to rate them as having a better ability to handle stress, plan, respond to reason, and exhibit self-control in frustrating situations. They could concentrate better without being easily distracted.

Funnily enough, the marshmallow study didn't end there. A few other researchers tracked down almost 60 people who are now middle-aged, who had previously been a part of the marshmallow experiment as young children. These psychologists proceeded to test the participants' willpower strength using a task that's been proven to prove self-control within adults. Surprisingly, the participants' various willpower strengths had been very consistent over the last 40 years. Overall, they found that the children who were not successful in resisting the first marshmallow did poorly on the self-control tasks as adults and that their hot stimuli seem to be consistent throughout their lifetime. They also began to study brain activity in some of the participants by using magnetic resonance technology. When they presented these participants with tempting stimuli, those with low willpower exhibited brain patterns that were very different from those with strong willpower. They discovered that the prefrontal cortex (this is the brain's region that controls choice-making functions) was more active in the participants who had stronger willpower. The ventral striatum (an area of the brain focused on processing rewards and desires) showed increased activity in the participants who had weaker willpower.

Common Myths About Willpower

The hot-cold framework does a great job of explaining people's ability to delay gratification. Still, another theory is called 'willpower depletion' that has emerged in recent years to explain what happens to people after they have resisted multiple temptations. Everyone exerts willpower every day in one form or another. People resist surfing the web or going on social media instead of finishing their work report. They may choose a salad when they are craving a slice of pizza. They may hold their tongue rather than make a snide remark. Recent growing research indicates that repeatedly resisting temptations takes a mental toll on a person. Some people describe willpower as a muscle that can get tired if overused.

The earliest discoveries of this concept came from a study conducted in Germany. The researcher brought participants into a room that smelled like fresh-baked cookies. The participants sat down at the table that held a bowl of radishes and a plate of those freshly baked cookies. The researchers asked some participants to taste those cookies while they asked others to try the radishes. After this, they asked the participants to complete a difficult geometric puzzle in 30 minutes. The researchers found that the participants who had to eat the radishes (therefore resisting the urge to eat the cookies) took 8 minutes to give up on the puzzle. In comparison, the participants who got to eat the cookies tried to complete the puzzle for 19 minutes. The evidence here seems as if the people who used their willpower to resist eating the cookies drained their resources for future situations.

This research was published in the late 90s, and since then, numerous other studies have begun looking into willpower depletion or otherwise known as ego depletion. For example, in one study, researchers asked participants to hold back and suppress any feelings they had while watching an emotional film. These participants then participated in a physical stamina test but gave up sooner than the participants who watched the movie and reacted normally without any suppression.

Depleting willpower is very common in today's society. You have probably tried to make yourself diplomatic when dealing with an aggravating customer or forced to fake happiness when your in-laws come to stay with you for an extended period. You must have realized that certain social interactions demand the use of willpower. There is also existing research proving that people interacting with others and maintaining relationships often is a high depleter of willpower.

Willpower depletion is not solely just a simple case of feeling tired. During another study by the same researcher, she had the participants in her study go through a whole day of sleep deprivation and then asked them to watch a movie and suppress their emotions and reactions during it. She then tested the strength of the participant's self-control and found that those participants who didn't get sleep were not much more likely to be depleted of willpower than those who got a full night's sleep.

So if willpower isn't related to physical fatigue, then what exactly is it? Research studies have recently discovered a few different mechanisms that are possibly responsible for willpower depletion, some that were at the biological level. The researchers found that the people whose willpower became depleted after completing self-control tasks showed lowered activity in the region of their brain that controlled cognition. When we test willpower, a person's brain may begin to function differently.

Some other evidence indicates that people who have depleted willpower might be low on fuel quite literally. Since the brain is an organ that requires high-energy and is powered by glucose, certain professionals suggested that the brain cells responsible for maintaining a person's self-control use up glucose quicker than they can replenish it. They performed a study with dogs where they asked obedient dogs to resist temptation showed lower blood glucose levels than the dogs that did not need to use self-control.

They found similar patterns in humans during scientific studies. The people who needed to use willpower in tasks showed lower glucose levels than the participants who weren't asked to utilize their willpower. Moreover, replenishing glucose levels tend to help reboot a depleted willpower source in individuals depleted while drinking a sugar-free drink.

However, evidence suggests that a person's attitudes and beliefs can maintain the depletion of willpower. Different research and other colleagues found out that the people who felt the need to use their willpower (usually to please other people) showed faster depletion of willpower than the people driven by their desires and goals. Therefore, these researchers suggested that the people who are in better touch with themselves may be better off in life compared to the people who are often people-pleasing.

Some other researchers also studied how the effects of mood could affect a person's willpower. A study in 2010 discovered that the group of people who believed that willpower is a limited resource was more likely to have willpower depletion. However, people who did not believe that willpower could be depleted didn't show any symptoms or signs of willpower exhaustion after using their self-control. During the next study stage, the psychologists manipulated the participants' subconscious beliefs by getting them to fill out a biased questionnaire unknowingly. The group that was manipulated to believe that willpower is, for a fact, a limited resource exhibited symptoms of willpower depletion/exhaustion. In contrast, the group that believed that willpower was not depletable didn't show any signs of declining self-control.

So at the end of all this evidence and discussion, do you think willpower is a limited resource? Many ideas point to evidence that supports both spectrums of this answer. They argued that willpower depletion in the early stages could be influenced by factors such as beliefs and mood. However, more research is required to explore how moods, attitudes, and beliefs might affect a person's ability to resist temptation.

Examples of the Benefits of Willpower

A person makes decisions every day to resist urges and gratification to seek a more healthy and happy long-term life. These urges could be in the form of refusing another portion of fries, forcing yourself to go work out, denying the second round of alcoholic drinks, or overcoming the temptation to skip early morning meetings. Willpower is being tested constantly within all of us.

Lack of willpower is often known as the main obstacle to people's ability to maintain a healthy weight and physique. A lot of research supports this idea. A study found that children with better self-control had less likelihood of becoming overweight when they grew up into their adolescent years due to their ability to delay gratification and control their urges.

However, just like we talked about earlier, resisting those urges may diminish a person's willpower to resist the next temptation. A researcher proved this in a study where they offered students that were currently dieting some ice cream after watching a sad movie. Researchers asked some of the participants to watch the movie like any other normal day, while the researchers asked the other group not to show any reactions or emotions, which is a task that requires self-control. The psychologists discovered that the participants who had to use their self-control to withhold their emotions and reactions indulged in more ice cream than the participants who were allowed to watch the movie normally and react as they'd like.

Many people often place most of the blame on their bad moods for causing their 'emotional eating.' However, that study found that the participants' emotional states were not the cause of the amount of ice cream they consumed. In layman's terms, the depletion of willpower had more significance than a person's mood when determining how much ice cream the participants ate.

We have to keep in mind that the reason behind why someone is on a diet will also play a role in willpower depletion. As we had just discussed, researchers found that people's attitudes and inner beliefs may create a buffer for them regarding the effects of willpower depletion. In a further study based on this theory, the researchers asked participants to resist the temptation of eating cookies that they placed in front of them. He then tested the participant's self-control strength by getting them to squeeze an exercise handgrip until they couldn't anymore. Through this exercise, he discovered that the people who refused to eat the cookies for their reasons (such as finding enjoyment in resisting treats) showed better control in this physical test compared to the ones who refused the cookies for reasons that were external (wanting to impress the experimenter).

At this point, it is obvious that willpower is a required component when it comes to eating healthy. If a person is living in a surrounding where there were plenty of unhealthy but delicious food options, the action of resisting temptation is more likely to deplete willpower and even making it difficult for highly motivated healthy eaters. Since overeating behaviors are very complex, the role of willpower is argumentative when it comes to discussions for obesity treatments.

Some of the experts in the field of willpower believe that using self-control and personal choices causes people to be stigmatized, making them unlikely to be motivated to lose weight. Many dieticians advise against using willpower as a tool and argue that dieters should be focusing on lowering the effect that their environment will have on their eating habits and behavior. Ultimately, when it comes to the world we live in today, resisting the temptation to eat unhealthily can be a hard challenge. We constantly see ads for delicious high-calorie foods. Cheap and fast processed foods are available at our fingertips 24/7 and are less expensive than healthier options. A person's willpower and the environment they live in play a big role in people's choices regarding food. Having a better understanding of both of these elements will help individuals and dieticians that are battling obesity.

Not only does willpower play a role in eating healthy, but it also plays a role in the use and possible abuse of alcohol, tobacco, and drugs. Children who have developed self-control may avoid substance abuse in their adulthood and teenagehood. Researchers in this field studied the self-control of adolescents as they moved from sixth grade to eleventh grade. They discovered that the kids who had self-control problems in sixth grades, such as not speaking in turn during class, had more likelihood of using tobacco, marijuana, and alcohol as high schoolers.

These results may not come as a surprise, but willpower also plays a significant role in curbing alcohol abuse and usage. In another study, a researcher discovered that people who drank socially often that used their willpower during the lab proceeded to go out and consume more alcohol than the other participants who didn't use their willpower stockpile. In a different study, the researcher found that the social drinkers who had used a lot of their self-control that day were more likely to infringe on the drinking limits that they created for themselves. This finding shows evidence that exerting self-control excessively in one situation can cripple a person's ability to fight off other temptations in different parts of their life.

We are talking a lot about willpower because understanding the role it plays is very important for developing effective treatments and planning to battle serious issues like addictions to help guide people in making healthier choices for themselves. Willpower research offers people lots of suggestions on how to stick with healthy behaviors.

Research Studies on Willpower in the Real World

The temptation of consumerism, including purchasing materialistic things like new shoes or a new car, is a test of willpower that we have all experienced. Like how unhealthy food options have become plentiful, the opportunities for impulse spending have grown. ATMs are on every corner, and the rise of online shopping only allows a person to spend all their money without having to even leave the comfort of their couch. Willpower depletion affects people's ability to choose healthier lifestyle options and also affects their purchasing behavior.

Professors from the University of Minnesota did a study that focused on impulse buying and willpower depletion. They showed the participants a silent movie with a series of words on the bottom of the screen. A group of those participants was asked not to pay attention to those words, which were a task that required the use of self-control. After the movie, they asked the participants to look through a catalog with products like cars and watches, and they wrote down the money amount that they were willing to pay for every single item. During the movie, the participants who used self-control were willing to spend more money, about $30,000, while the participants who didn't deplete their willpower were willing to spend approximately $23,000.

In the next experiment, the researchers tested the participants' spending behavior by showing them the opportunity to buy lower-cost objects like cups and decorative stickers. The group that had done self-control in the previous experiment expressed a higher temptation to buy those items. They purchased more items and spent more money than the participants who hadn't done the self-control exercise.

The task of making financial decisions can be much harder for impoverished people. Researchers conducted various studies in India to explore the relationship between poverty and will power strength. This researcher visited two different villages in one study, one poor village and one rich village. The researcher offered people an opportunity to buy a luxury brand name soap at an extremely discounted price tag. This item was a great deal in terms of cost, but it still showed that people who live in poverty had difficulty making financial decisions.

They asked the study participants to squeeze a handgrip made for exercise, a popular test of strength regarding self-control, before and after they offered the soap to be purchased. The researcher found that the participants who had more money exercised the handgrip for the same time before and after-experiment. The experiment involved the opportunity to buy that soap. However, they found that poor participants squeezed the handgrip for a smaller amount of time after purchasing decisions. Their willpower was depleted, and the researcher concluded that the difficulty likely depleted it of making that financial decision.

This research may sound depressing, but there is a silver lining. Suppose impoverished people have a higher chance of using up their willpower. In that case, it could mean that lowering the number of hard decisions that they have to make every day to help prevent the depletion of willpower will allow them to make future decisions. A different researcher studied this effect amongst thanking customers in Southeast Asia. They offered customers the opportunity to open a savings account, but it comes with a catch. These customers would only be able to withdraw their funds after reaching a targeted saving goal or target date that they have decided for themselves. A year later, the participants that signed up for these accounts saved 82% more than the participants who had not opened the special savings account. When the decision to either save money or spend money is removed, it helps customers avoid self-control.

All of this evidence collaborated to show that the people who are in the lower end of the socioeconomic spectrum are more likely to deplete their self-control resources. It's not that people who don't have money have less willpower than rich people; rather, the people living in poverty have to make more willpower draining decisions. This result shows that every decision they make, whether it is as simple as buying soap, will require self-control, which, therefore, dips into their limited resources of willpower.

CHAPTER 3
Motivation

In this chapter, we will be looking at why having self-discipline is more important than motivation. A common excuse that people use regarding their low-self-discipline is, "I don't have any motivation to do this right now; I'll wait until I feel motivated to do this task." This chapter will help you move past this mindset and into one where you focus less on your motivation levels and move on to how to create motivation for yourself by doing your tasks.

To begin, I will define the term *motivation* for you. Motivation is different for every person, in every scenario, but it is possible to reduce this to a single definition for this term. Motivation is something within a person that drives the wish to change something about their life. Motivation, then, comes down to wanting something that you do not have. These desired changes can be internal or external- in a person's environment. Motivation combines with the desire to change to make a person take action and steps toward their desired outcomes. Motivation is what helps people accomplish things that they set out to do. Some motivation is triggered by needs, like the need to sustain your life (eating, sleeping, etc.), and some are triggered by needs of a psychological nature, like the need for human connection.

Throughout this book, we will revisit the term motivation repeatedly to help you ensure the most success possible. By examining your motivations, you will be likely to stay on track. Understanding your motivations for something that you wish to achieve helps you remember why you began and helps you push through when things become difficult.

The Difference Between Motivation and Discipline

People often have the wrong mindset where they think that they need to feel fully motivated before they start working on a task/job. This mindset is unrealistic.

People's motivation often does not arrive until they have started that task and are beginning to see progress. When people see progress, they start to see the fruits of their labor, and they become even more motivated to keep working until they have completed their task. You might be wondering, what about the motivation that is needed to start working altogether? Before you even begin working on it, you should know what the benefits are going to be. You would be surprised at how many people waste a lot of time doing work that they do not need to do.

Moreover, people should be using prioritization to get the most urgent and important work out of the way first. By understanding the benefits of completing a task or job, you will fully estimate its importance. In terms of smaller tasks/jobs, simply understanding the benefits of completing that task should be enough for motivation. For larger tasks and jobs, you must have a way to measure your progress to gain motivation and confidence from your work further.

One main reason people put off doing the work they need to do is that they subconsciously find that their work is too overwhelming. Start by just breaking down whatever that task is into littler parts and then focus on one at a time. If you find yourself still wanting to procrastinate after you've already broken it down, then break it down even more. You will eventually get to a point where the task you need to do is so easy that you would feel very badly about yourself if you didn't just do it.

For example, imagine that one of your goals is to manage your money better. It is tax season, and you need to complete your taxes to understand your financial situation. Imagine that you are feeling overwhelmed as you don't even know where to begin filing your taxes. You are also afraid that you may owe money to the government that you might not have. Here is how I would break down the large and broad task of 'filing taxes':

1. Research the best way to file taxes for beginners
2. Explore my options (either downloading software for DIY or going to a tax filing company)
3. Pick which option suits you best
4. Gather the documents that are suggested based on which option you chose in step #2
5. Follow the instructions given to you by the tax software or the tax professional

Suddenly that one large task of 'filing taxes' became much more manageable. Instead of thinking about filing taxes as one large unit, you are now starting with a simple google search of the best way to file taxes for beginners. From there, now you can make an educated decision on which method is easiest for you. By taking things one step at a time, your mind becomes less overwhelmed.

The Relationship Between Self-Discipline and Motivation

In this section, we will look at the relationship between self-discipline and motivation in a little more detail now that you understand what motivation is and how it works.

Understanding the psychology behind self-discipline is extremely crucial as it will help you learn what the driving factors are behind having and increasing it.

Interestingly, one of the main factors that drive self-discipline is willpower. Earlier in this book, we learned about willpower and how it can be improved and developed. Remember that a common belief in people is that they think they can change their lives for the better if they simply could have more willpower. Charles Duhigg is a prize-winning author who covers the subject of 'The Power of Habit.' Some of the topics and concepts that he discovered in his book are concerned with how willpower is not as important if you can develop good habits and develop your self-discipline. This point is similar to motivation and how motivation is less important than self-discipline.

In this way, you can see that willpower, motivation, and discipline are all related. Having a high level of self-discipline is much more important than having intrinsic motivation or having the willpower to complete your tasks.

CHAPTER 4
Goal Setting

We will use this chapter to discuss goal setting in-depth to take your knowledge of self-discipline a little bit further and help you improve it. I'm going to provide you with a few more tips and habits that will help you strengthen your self-discipline and help you achieve everything you want in life.

Goal setting is the first action that a person needs to make to reach their goals. The purpose of setting a goal is so that a person can achieve their desired results. When a goal is set carefully with focus, momentum, action, and intention, setting and achieving goals is the first step a person needs to take to move from where they are not to where they want to be. However, they need to know where they want to be—the "where" begins with a person envisioning it.

A Vision Versus a Goal

In this section, before we proceed, we will look at the difference between a vision and a goal. This distinction will help you when trying to create your own goals for yourself.

I will begin by defining a vision. A vision is something that exists within a person that is internally sourced. A person simply needs to get in touch with their vision, as it comes from within. A person's vision is the big picture of the desired outcomes they have for their life. It represents the most important things to that person and is often compelling, inspiring, exciting, and filled with many positive emotions.

A goal, on the other hand, is different. You specifically design a goal, which requires a set of tasks to complete to reach it. A goal is designed by a person that will help them ultimately reach their vision. The downside here is that a person's goal may not initiate those positive emotions that become an inspiration as their vision does. Goals are more like stepping stones on a path that will lead you to your ultimate end goal, whereas a vision is something that does not come with a set of steps along the way.

Finding Your "Why"

Our discussion of a person's vision leads us to the topic of "finding the reason why." To continue strengthening your self-discipline, a person must have a clear vision of what they are trying to accomplish. They must also have an understanding of what success means to them. If a person doesn't know where they're planning to go or what achieving their goals even entails, it is easy for them to lose their way or get sidetracked. We call this act *finding the reason why,* which is what will inspire you every day to continue working towards the goals you have set for yourself.

The first step to this is to start imaging the end in mind and work backward (this is what we discussed in the visualization chapter. Many people mistake their goal for vision thinking when the goal is the result. They will set a goal without thinking about what the goal will allow them to do, be, or have in the long term. To make the most out of your goal-setting process, it is essential to think about what quality of lifestyle they want to achieve ultimately. For clarity, let's talk a little bit more between a person's vision and their goal.

One way that people can achieve this is by using imagery that is vivid and highly detailed. This practice can be a very powerful way for someone to train their minds to go after the things they want. Athletes often use visualization to help themselves train. For example, famous golf athlete Tiger Woods has been using visualization to help train his golfing techniques ever since he was a teenager. Even the NBA star Michael Jordan used mental imagery to help get himself into the mindset that he wants to make his famous three-point shots. If professional athletes use visualization techniques, they can enhance their ability to be the best. You can also use visualization and meditation to help you achieve your goals and increase your self-discipline level.

How to Set Goals for Yourself

In this section, we are going to begin talking about how you can set goals for yourself.

Setting attainable goals is more effective than setting Broad and large goals. Setting smaller goals becomes more quantifiable, and because of this, you can easily keep track of how you are doing when it comes to goal achievement.

Active goal setting differs greatly from passive goal-setting. Passive goal setting means you are setting goals within your head, and they are passive because they don't have enough details. Passive goal-setting means that a person hasn't properly defined the actual goal, making it hard for them to keep track of their progress and keep track of what they need to do to achieve that goal. Active goal setting is the complete opposite of passive goal-setting. Active goal setting means writing out these goals and making sure that they have an important meeting. These goals have to be measurable and very specific. To successfully have an active goal, a person has to make a plan towards achieving it. This plan is why people set long-term goals and engage in smaller goals daily to achieve a bigger goal.

Active goal setting works by taking the first step in setting your long-term goals. Suppose you have long-term goals like; wanting to own your first home, wanting to pay off your student debt by the next three years, or taking six months off to travel Europe. If you have long-term goals, you need to actively participate in daily, weekly, and monthly goal setting and planning. You have to play an active role in tracking your progress towards your goals and making changes in places where you feel like you aren't working.

So take some time to yourself and start writing down what long-term goals you have. Once you have some long-term goals written down, break it down into monthly, weekly, and daily goals. Start slowly by accomplishing your daily goals, and when you reach the end of the month, assess to see if you have achieved your monthly goal through accomplishing your daily goals. If you haven't, look back on your daily goals and see if there's anything you can change to achieve next month's goal.

Using active goal-setting ingrains the discipline in people because you must give your goals a direction. By breaking down your big goals into smaller daily goals, it helps people avoid distractions by only looking at what they need to get done in the present day. This way, a person isn't left constantly thinking about one large intimidating goal but not knowing how to approach it.

The most popular and effective way to build your goals is using the SMART goals format. You may have done or heard of this before at your workplace or while you were in school. SMART stands for specific, measurable, achievable, resources, and time. This acronym helps you make sure that your goals are specific and concise, you have a way of measuring them, achievable goals, have or have a way of getting the necessary resources, and have a timeline in which you want to achieve your goals.

SMART stands for the following acronym;
- Specific

This part of the acronym will help you make sure that your goals are specific and concise enough to know what you are working towards with no confusion or ambiguity.

- Measurable

The "M" in the acronym ensures that you have a way of measuring your goals to be aware of exactly when you reach your goals. This measurement will also help you determine how far you are from achieving your goals, as you can measure where you are now and where you want to be when you reach your goal.

- Achievable

The "A" ensures that you set goals that are achievable for you. Achievable means that you are setting goals that consider where you are starting from and how far you can get in the amount of time you have set out for yourself.

For instance, if you hope to lose weight, it would not be achievable to set a goal such as, "I want to lose 10 pounds in one week." There is no healthy way to do this, so this would not be an achievable goal. Since the recommended healthy maximum amount of weight loss is roughly one

pound per week, it would be better to set yourself a goal like, "I want to lose 6 pounds in 6 weeks," or something such as this.
- Resources / Realistic

This part of the acronym ensures that you have a way of getting the necessary resources required for you to reach your goals. These resources could be anything from financial resources to a support system or any other resources you would need to reach your goals. It is important to take this into account to adjust your goals accordingly or so that you can figure out what you need to reach those goals. The second half to this letter in the acronym is that the goals are realistic. This point is similar to the "Achievable" step, as we learned above. Still, in this case, you must give yourself a reality check to ensure that you can achieve your goal and that you will not leave yourself disappointed by setting yourself up for failure.
- Time

The acronym's final letter represents having a timeline in which you want to achieve your goals. This timeline will give you the much-needed sense of urgency that will help you continue making progress toward your goals day in and day out, without feeling as though you have all the time in the world, which could lead you to avoid making progress toward your goals. On the other hand, you do not want to set your goals on a too short timeline, as this could lead them to become unrealistic or unachievable if there is too little time for you to take the necessary steps to reach your goals.

Using this acronym to set your goals will help you ensure that you are setting goals that you can achieve, and that will set you on the path to success by helping you build momentum as you achieve short-term goals on the way to achieving your long-term goals.

For example, make sure the goals that you are setting have a clear and concise purpose. For example, don't use goals like "I want to be rich by the next five years." This goal is too broad for it to have a strong meaning. Instead, you should make a goal that is quantifiable like "I am planning on saving $20,000 by the end of this year". Then, when you have a quantifiable goal, you can make a plan that makes sense for yourself. In this example, a person can plan to save $2,000 each month for the rest of this year to hit their goal of saving $20,000 by the end of it. They can break down these goals even further and figure out where they can save money or how they can make more money to accomplish that goal in their budget.

Tips for Setting Goals That You Can Achieve

Make sure the goals that you are setting have a clear and concise purpose. For example, don't use goals like "I want to be rich by the next five years." This goal is too broad for it to have a strong meaning. Instead, you should make a goal that is quantifiable like "I am planning on saving $20,000 by the end of this year". Then, when you have a quantifiable goal, you can make a plan that makes sense for yourself. In this example, the person can break down these goals even further and figure out where they can save money or how they can make more money to accomplish that goal in their budget.

Whatever your objective, writing it down will help to solidify it and make it more real. By having it written down on paper, you will have put your reason for doing all of this out into the universe, and it will make you feel as if there is no going back now. This action will keep you motivated when times get tough. You can revisit that paper anytime you need a reminder of why you are taking on such a challenge. Seeing that paper will remind you of why it is all worth it. If you begin wondering, "why on earth did I decide to put myself through this?" as you begin to incorporate new behaviors into your daily routine, you can look back on your reasons for choosing to begin in the first place (that you wrote down), and they will re-inspire you to continue. This mindset will enable you to keep going even when you feel as though it is difficult, leading to lasting changes. When it comes to mindset, being aware of your motivation is extremely beneficial.

Surrounding yourself with people that can encourage you and foster positivity will also change your inner-critic's opinion. Often, hearing positive compliments from other people holds a heavier weight in the eyes of your inner-critic compared to you telling your inner-critic the same thing. Try spending time with people who support your goals and the changes you are looking to make in your life. It will make your journey a little bit easier.

By limiting your life's negative influences, you are making a statement that you place importance on preserving your mental health. When you remove negative forces and limit your exposure to things or people that make you feel negative, you prioritize yourself, which is a great way to practice self-care.

Adopting helpful thought processes fosters better emotions overall, which leads to more productive behaviors.

When people have developed unhelpful thinking processes, it is hard for them to make decisions that will benefit their future selves because their thoughts create negative emotions that drive away motivation. In this case, is where something called *positive self-talk* can come in. Positive self-talk can be instrumental in helping you to practice self-discipline and achieve your goals.

The inner critic controls many people's minds. The inner critic shares words with you, such as "You should just give up" Or "What makes you think you'll succeed?" which is rooted in the opposite of positive self-talk- Negative self-talk! Instead of creating an open space that allows for mistakes, growth, and development, your inner critic causes you to question your worth. AS a result, this makes it difficult for you to have the positive, growth mindset that you need to complete tasks and go after things that may be difficult to achieve. In this case, helping your mind begin using positive self-talk will help you recover for the long-term. You must learn how to combat this to move forward in your life and find success.

How Visualization Can Help You

One of the most powerful and inspiring things that humans can do is visualize the things that they want to manifest and then actually make it happen. The human mind's power is extraordinary, especially when it is coupled with mindfulness practices like meditation. Using meditation, a person can increase their ability and make heaps of progress towards the life they want to create.

What Is Visualization?

Many athletes in individual sports use the act of visualization to help themselves train before a competition. For example, in Olympic cycling, the cyclist will prepare for a game by closing their eyes and visualizing the racetrack in their mind. They move their bodies while imagining how they will travel through the racetrack to train their muscle memory and reflexes even further. This way, when they do begin to compete on the racetrack, they have already visualized themselves cycling through it using the strategies that they have been taught and visualized in their minds. This technique is a skill that many professional coaches teach their athletes to do.

When a person is visualizing, their conscious mind is aware that what they're visualizing is not real but is just a result of imagination. Consequently, a person's subconscious cannot differentiate between what a person is thinking and what they are doing. In other words, a person's inner mind isn't able to distinguish the difference between real life, a photo, memories, or an imagined future. Instead, the mind is under the impression that everything a person sees is real. Numerous brain scans that scientists have conducted over the years have proven this fact. They discovered that there are no brain activity differences when someone observes something in the real world compared to when a person is visualizing.

All of this evidence is extremely important because it points to the theory that visualization can help people learn new skills and reprogram and rewire their brains without performing physical actions. For example, if somebody is looking to increase their self-esteem, they can use visualization by imagining themselves doing those actions before actually doing it in the real world.

How to Use Visualization

This visualization technique is the most important one when it comes to strengthening self-discipline. Using the visualization technique for setting goals brings a lot of value, but this technique does come with one major drawback. The most popular form of visualization is goal setting. Most people have used visualization of their goals at one time or another. However, this technique may not have worked for them due to one critical flaw. This flaw is that when people visualize their goals, they only focus on visualizing their end goal and nothing in between. They see within their mind's a big and flashy awesome goal that's going to be rainbows and butterflies. Yes, they are experiencing this using all of their senses, but they simply open their eyes after the visualization feeling very inspired. However, this type of motivation is extremely short-lived because the next time this person faces an obstacle, it immediately deflates their motivation.

When this happens, people feel they visualize their goal again to create more motivation. However, because nothing happens every time they visualize their goal, their motivation doesn't grow either. Every time a person hits an obstacle, and they try the process of visualization again, their motivation becomes weaker every time, and they start to lose more and more energy.

The mistake that these people are making is that they are not properly visualizing their goals. They only see the destination, but they don't understand that achieving a goal takes much more than just that. Achieving a goal is part of a journey that is full of emotional highs and lows, wins and losses, and a journey of ups and downs. Due to this, these are the things that a person would also need to include in their visualization.

When a person visualizes their end goal, it is very effective in creating that desire and hunger. However, the proper way to use visualization is to spend 10 percent of your time visualizing the end goal and spending the rest of the visualization time thinking about HOW you will achieve your goals and overcome challenges. In some ways, it's similar to the form of visualization planning that we just discussed.

A person's end goal helps keep inspiration running in the long term, but it is the journey that helps a person stay motivated in the short term. To maximize the time spent on achieving small goals to get to your end goal, you must visualize those as well.

Below are five steps that you can follow to achieve this visualization:
1. Get yourself to a quiet place and sit down and close your eyes. Start to visualize your end goal. Imagine yourself experiencing and living this goal using all five of your senses.
2. Slowly take steps backward from your end goal and visualize the process that you took that lead to you achieving your end goal.

Imagine all the problems you faced that put you back; however, you can see yourself finding solutions to those problems. Continue visualizing until you are back to the present moment.
3. Now, move forward with time and visualize how you took on opportunities that helped you overcome your problems.
4. At the end of this visualization, take a few moments to send your future self some positive energy for their journey.
5. When you exit the visualization, emotionally detach from the outcome of your goal. The thing that can hold you back is to have an emotional attachment to a specific result. Instead, try to stay open-minded and be flexible for what's to come on your journey.

You can use visualization using those steps on a daily or weekly basis. Weekly sessions can be as long as 30 minutes, and you can keep your daily sessions shorter, so they are between 5 - 10 minutes. However, be sure that you are using your daily sessions to visualize the next steps of achieving your goal for the upcoming week. This visualization will help you continue moving forward to reach your goal.

CHAPTER 5
Procrastination

Procrastination is self-discipline's worst enemy. Understanding the process of procrastination will help you better overcome this hurdle that many people face. The purpose of this chapter is to give you a detailed look into what exactly procrastination is, the psychology behind it, reasons why people procrastinate, bust some common myths, and learn about some of the long-term consequences of procrastination. The modern definition of procrastination is "the act of delaying or postponing a task or set of tasks." Let's learn a little about why people procrastinate. What exactly is going on in the human brain that causes people to avoid doing what they KNOW they should be doing?

What Is Procrastination?

Through an abundance of psychology research, psychologists have discovered a phenomenon called "time inconsistency," which helps explain why procrastination affects humans so largely by pulling us away from needed tasks despite our good intentions. The term time inconsistency refers to the human mind's habit to value immediate gratification or rewards more highly compared to long-term and future rewards. The best way to further understand this is to imagine that you have two alter egos. The first is your present self, and the second is your future self. When a person sets goals for themselves, such as getting fit by working out more or learning a new language, they make plans for their future self. They are envisioning what they want their life to be like in the future. Evidence has shown researchers that when a person thinks about their future self, it is not difficult for their brain to see the value of doing actions that will lead to long-term benefits. The future self is the one that values long-term rewards.

On the contrary, while the future self can only set goals, the present self is the one that is responsible for taking action. There will come a time where this individual will need to decide, but they aren't choosing the future self. In the present moment, their brain is focused entirely on the present self. Research shows that the present self prefers immediate rewards over long-term ones. This research finding means that the present self and future self don't often get along. While the future self wants to be healthy and have a six pack, the present self wants some chili cheese fries. Everyone knows that eating unhealthy will prevent health problems in the future when you're at an old age, but those things are so far away, so why worry about them now, right? This thought process occurs when you face a choice of immediate gratification or achieving long-term goals.

Similarly, most young people know that saving money for their retirement during their 20s and 30s is extremely valuable, but the benefit of this is many decades away. It is much easier for a person's present-self to see value in buying themselves a new iPhone rather than putting away $1000 for their 75-year-old self! This concept of "time inconsistency" may be the reason why people often go to bed feeling motivated and inspired to reach their goals and change their life. Still, they find themselves completely falling back into bad habits when they wake up. This relapse happens because the human brain values long-term benefits when thinking about the future, but it prefers immediate gratification when it comes to the present moment. Let's dive into a little bit more of the science behind this.

For the sake of example here, let's pretend for a little while that you are a giraffe living in the plains of the African savanna. Your neck is 6 feet long, and occasionally you will see a group of human tourists driving in a car with a safari tour taking pictures of you. However, it's not just your long neck that separates you from the humans. It could be that the biggest difference between you and your other giraffe friends and the humans taking pictures is that almost every single decision that you make brings an immediate benefit to your life. For example, when you see a storm coming, you will find shelter under a tree, or if you are hungry, you walk over to the nearest tree and begin to eat, or when you spot a predator hunting you, you begin to run away.

Every day, most of the choices you make as a giraffe, like where to sleep, how to avoid predators, or what to eat, make a direct and immediate impact on your life. You would be entirely focused on the present moment, and the furthest ahead you would look is into the near future. You live in an 'Immediate-Return Environment'; this is what scientists call this environment since your actions deliver very immediate and clear outcomes.

Now let's change things up and pretend that you are one of the human tourists traveling in Africa on the safari. Different from giraffes, humans live in a 'Delayed Return Environment.' Most of the choices made in this type of environment will not benefit you right away. For example, if you save your money now, you'll have enough for retirement in forty years, or if you work hard at your job today, you will get paid in two weeks. Rewards will be delayed until some point in the future in many aspects of modern-day society.

While the giraffe is worried about immediate problems, such as avoiding predators, seeking shelters, and finding food, humans worry the most about the future's problems. For instance, while the humans are on the safari, they may be thinking, "This trip and safari has been tremendous fun! It would be so awesome if I could work as a safari tour guide and be able to see the giraffes every day. Speaking of work, is it time for me to change my career? Am I working on the kind of job that I enjoy? Should

I start looking for new jobs?" Unfortunately for us, humans living in a Delayed Return Environment tend to lead to a lot of anxiety and stress. This reason for this is because the human brain wasn't designed to solve problems of a Delayed Return Environment.

For this reason, there has been a rise in depression and anxiety over the last decade. People of the past focused more on their immediate problems like harvesting their crops for food or boiling water, so it's safe to drink. People nowadays focus on problems in the future since most of our basic needs are already taken care of for us.

The Most Common Causes of Procrastination

Now that we know that all of life in a Delayed Return Environment, let's learn a little about why people procrastinate. Most people are more than capable of achieving great things in their life, but many fail to do so. Procrastination is probably one of the biggest obstacles that hinder a person from achieving greater things. Everyone has procrastinated before, and anyone is capable of it. Many times, people don't even know that they are procrastinating. However, there are also those moments where people know that they are procrastinating but fail to stop the process. So why do people procrastinate anyways, although they are self-aware? There are numerous reasons why people begin procrastinating; let's take a look at the most common ones:

1. Skill Deficiency

For a person to achieve their goals, it requires them to learn and to have personal growth. People will have to develop new skills and knowledge related to the goals they want to achieve. This knowledge acquisition is a huge part of their journey. However, people often fail to see this fact. They see their lack of skill or knowledge as an obstacle that is permanent and as something that they cannot overcome. This mindset causes people to give up on their goals before they have even done anything to start it. Rather than giving up, people need to assess the skills and knowledge required to achieve their goal and then compare it to their skills and knowledge that they possess. The difference between the two is nothing more than just an opportunity to learn and train. Instead of just giving up, people need to create a plan that will help them develop and learn the skills needed to bridge that gap. So is it procrastination if you are pushing the date of your goal back? No. This exercise is just effective for planning. Understanding that you require more time to reach your goal means that you are identifying the right steps you need to take to reach your goal.

2. Lack of interest

Everyone has their own special set of interests. Just because your friend is passionate about a particular topic or job, it does not mean that everyone else is interested in the same thing. People tend to put off doing jobs that they do not find interesting because it is more difficult to find motivation. There are multiple ways that people can deal with jobs that they have no interest in depending on whether you are the person who is doing the job or the person who is simply assigning the task. Let's take a look at the perspective of a person that is physically doing the job; they could try the following things:

- Check to see if this task has to be done.
- Ask yourself if there is someone else who is much better suited to completing this task. If possible, you may be able to swap it or delegate it (e.g., if someone else likes that job better, you can trade with that person for the job you might like better)
- If your tolerance for frustration is low, try to break down this job into smaller pieces and complete them one at a time.
- If your tolerance for frustration is higher, you can schedule a block of time to remove all distractions and just do this task until you complete it.

From the perspective of the person who is assigning the job/task, you will likely find more success if you assign this specific task to someone whom you know will be passionate about it. By choosing someone interested in that task, they will complete the job in a much faster fashion and at a higher standard.

3. Lack of motivation

People often have the wrong mindset where they think that they need to feel fully motivated before they start working on a task/job. This mindset is unrealistic. People's motivation often does not arrive until they have started that task and is beginning to see progress. When people see progress, they start to see the fruits of their labor, and they become even more motivated to keep working until they have completed their task. You might be wondering, what about the motivation that is needed to start working altogether? The answer to this is the following; a person needs to have a solid understanding of why they want to achieve their goal. Before you even begin working on it, you should know what the benefits are going to be. You would be surprised at how many people waste a lot of time doing work they do not need to complete.

Moreover, people should be using prioritization to get the most urgent and important work out of the way first. By understanding the benefits of completing a task or job, you will fully estimate its importance. In terms of smaller tasks/jobs, simply understanding the benefits of completing that task should be enough for motivation. For larger tasks and jobs, you must have a way to measure your progress to gain motivation and confidence from your work further.

4. Fear of failure

There are a lot of people who have the belief that failure is devastating. They often see failure as a final result set in stone and cannot be rectified or changed. Failure to them is a permanent stain on their reputation, which means that every time that they fail, their ego takes a huge hit. This lack of confidence causes them to avoid taking action on tasks where they are not 100% confident in its success. Keep in mind that in the era that we live in today, many tasks that people face will be new to them, and it is entirely impossible to be able to be 100% confident in every single chance of success. Due to this, procrastination is something that happens frequently and in an endless spiral.

On the contrary, the people out there see failure as a stepping stone towards success and a learning opportunity. They understand and believe that mistakes are unavoidable and that they will inevitably make mistakes along the way. Their attitude consists mostly of realistic optimism, which enables them to believe that they will successfully achieve their goal/task even if it's something that requires more than one try. As you might be able to tell, these types of people have a much lower tendency to procrastinate. Instead, they often approach new challenges with excitement and preparedness to deal with obstacles.

Since learning and growth are important parts of a successful life, it is unrealistic to believe that you can succeed without experiencing any obstacles or failures in your journey. If you are constantly worrying and are scared at the idea of failure, try to identify extra steps or measures that you can take to lower the chances of failure and increase the chances of success. You must factor in the time it can take to review and assess your actions and learn something from every experience. You will soon start to change your mindset into one where you see every challenge as an opportunity for learning and growth.

5. Fear of success

Many professionals of the self-help industry have talked or theorized about the fact that people's biggest fear wasn't necessarily a failure. Still, our biggest fear is the fear of success. Many people view success as stress and pressure. When they think about achieving greater and more things, they often think about the negative aspects that come with it. For example, they believe that people will begin to demand and expect more from you when a person achieves more. They often doubt their ability to deal with the increased expectations, so they decide to procrastinate to sabotage their chances of success.

The reality here is that there is no reason that a person should fear success. As a person begins to succeed by overcoming all difficulties, they begin to become more knowledgeable and have developed new skills. Their resilience will begin to increase. If a person can learn the necessary skills of personal organization, it doesn't matter what type of task or work they are doing; they will be able to find a way through. Long story short, every task is simply just a task that they need to complete. When you can break down every large task into several smaller tasks, there should be nothing that would be able to overwhelm you.

6. Resistance

You might have experienced this phenomenon before, where there are times that it would be easier for you just to complete a task than procrastinate but yet you still chose to procrastinate! The main reason for this is rebellion. There is a class of procrastinators called the 'rebellious procrastinators'; they are very common. These people deliberately delay tasks, defy standards, falter expectations, and impedes protocol. This type of procrastination can be done by anyone, especially if they feel like they have been mistreated.

The reasons that cause people to procrastinate are different for every individual. The exact reason why each individual does it may not be obvious, but underlying issues may cause procrastination. On the contrary, the reasons that we have just discussed are the most common ones. Trying to avoid this type of behavior is not an easy task as it often involves a person to identify their bad habits and actively try to break them down and create new ones. Whether you are the procrastinator or suffering at the hands of one, the important part here is to take action immediately. You have to take action to correct your situation. Keep in mind that procrastination is a serious issue that can cause some serious and long-lasting problems in your life if left unresolved for a long time.

The Most Common Excuses Used for Procrastination

Let's begin to learn about some of the most common excuses and myths regarding procrastination. By learning about what these are, we can get those false ideas out of our minds and focus on facts. There are numerous myths and excuses that people tell themselves to avoid doing the work that they need to do. Below are four of the most common myths regarding procrastination.

1. "I need to be inspired or feeling motivated before I can begin working."

People often put off doing certain tasks until they're 'in the mood' or 'feeling inspired.' By telling yourself that you are waiting for a certain emotion to come is just procrastination in disguise. Rather than waiting for a certain emotion to come before getting started on your task/work, you instead tell yourself that you must do this work, regardless of how much inspiration you feel. By doing this, you will find that inspiration is a product of discipline. When you begin to start working on the task you've set, you will start feeling fulfilled, leading to actual inspiration. Simply just stop wasting time waiting for the feeling of inspiration to hit you. Just like Picasso once said, "Inspiration exists, but it has to find you working."

2. "I work better under pressure."

Think about this for a second; imagine that you have an important work report due to your boss in two weeks. Instead of starting the report, you find yourself doing other unnecessary things like reorganizing your stamp collection or cleaning your bathtub. To reduce the disagreement between what you should be doing and what you are doing, you start to rationalize your behavior. You begin telling yourself that you are just the type of person who works better 'under pressure' so the best thing that you can do for yourself is to delay the start of your report.

The hard reality here is that procrastination is harmful to a person's performance. Last-minute scrambling around to get tasks and jobs done or cramming the night before a final exam is not efficient or enjoyable. When people plan and pace their projects, it typically gets them better results, and it is a lot less stressful than pulling all-nighters to get things done. If you convince yourself that you can't start working on a task unless you feel the pressure of a close deadline, you can try to fix this habit by creating artificial pressure for yourself. There are a few ways that you can approach this technique. For instance, you can set a 30-minute timer and tell yourself that you only have 30 minutes to write your report's opening paragraph. You can convince yourself that you are being timed while you write the report you have to complete and that at the end of the 30-minute timer, you have to stop writing. You could also try asking a friend to be your 'accountability buddy' to whom you have to 'hand in' your work.

3. "I need to have at least 3 – 4 hours of uninterrupted time to work on this."

People often believe in the myth that they need a certain huge chunk of uninterrupted time to accomplish whatever they are looking to accomplish. However, if a person doesn't have a long chunk of time to work on their task, such as that report that's due in two weeks, they are making a mistake by delaying their task until they find themselves with a few hours of uninterrupted time. Rather than doing this, you should try to apply a technique called the "Swiss Cheese Approach." Swiss cheese is a type of cheese famous for its numerous holes; thus, the Swiss cheese approach means that a person can get something started in just 5 minutes or less. Once a person has started, they have opened up their opportunity to keep it going.

The Swiss Cheese Approach comprises the following elements:
• Try working in small 'holes' of time. Try getting some work done in just 15, 20, or 30 minutes.
• Work away at large tasks by poking small 'holes' consistently.

This approach is efficient because of these reasons:
• Once you start working on a task, it no longer feels as overwhelming or difficult as before.

- By poking small 'holes' in a task you're doing, you'll make little but constant progress.
- This approach will help you build a sense of 'forward momentum'; you are motivated to keep doing more once you start.
- Each time you complete a small amount of the task you need to do, it will give you a sense of accomplishment.
- You are making good use of small portions of time rather than wasting it completely.

The next time you find yourself with only 15 – 20 minutes to work on your task/project, rather than telling yourself that you don't have enough time or waiting until you have a longer time block, ask yourself these questions below:

- "Is there a small 'hole' in this project that I can start with?"
- "How can I use this time to poke a small 'hole' in my task?"
- "What can I get done in 10 – 15 minutes?"

By continuing to poke 'holes' into your tasks and projects whenever you find yourself with some time to spare, you will be surprised to find that you have accomplished a lot of your task.

4. "I'll be able to do this job better tomorrow."

Everyone tends to believe that things will be different in the future, even if the 'future' means tomorrow. The mindset is often, "In the future, I'll have more time and organize myself better. In the future, I'll have more energy and be more well-rested, so I can get things done." Due to this, people often pass over their present-day responsibilities over to their future selves, not knowing that they probably won't be that much different from now. Here are a few items that you need to consider; firstly, unless you actively start taking action needed to be more effective and productive right now, you'll be in the same situation tomorrow. Second, unless you are doing the necessary actions to increase your discipline in the present moment, you will be just as undisciplined tomorrow. Lastly, unless you are taking steps to become more organized right now, you will be at the same level of disorganization tomorrow. We can summarize all of this in just one sentence; don't put off things for tomorrow that you can do today.

Almost all of us have at least truly believed in one of those four myths as a way to be excused from completing tasks/work that didn't make us feel comfortable. It could be because we fear doing a bad job, or that task seemed too complex, or we were feeling overwhelmed, or simply just because there was something else 'better' to do.

How to Overcome Procrastination Using Self-Discipline

Procrastination is often something that impacts those with low self-discipline. However, we learned that motivation is something that happens after you take action rather than before. To overcome procrastination, you can't sit around waiting for motivation to hit; you have to begin your task to create motivation. To start doing a task without motivation, you need to utilize your willpower and self-discipline. Let's take a look at 11 steps that we can take to overcome procrastination and begin creating motivation for ourselves. The first step is to break down a big goal into littler ones, which we learned in the previous chapter. We'll start this guide at the second step.

- Step 2: Optimize Your Environment

Different types of environments produce different impacts on a person's productivity. Take a look at your workspace, does looking at it make you want to go back to bed? Or does it look inviting enough to make you want to jump right into work? If it's the former, you may want to consider changing up your workspace to make it more inviting. For instance, I used to have stronger procrastination feelings when I allowed my desk to get cluttered. It did not look inviting, and in fact, it added stress as now I needed to clear up my workspace before doing a task that I didn't even really want to do in the first place. By keeping your workspace clean, tidy, and inviting, you can skip the step of having to tidy up before getting your hands dirty with work.

- Step 3: Develop A Plan That Has Details And Deadlines

When a person just has one singular deadline for a large task, it's an invitation to procrastinate. This procrastination happens because people get under the impression that they have time and continue to keep pushing things back until the deadline is looming over them. In step one, we discussed breaking down your task into smaller ones. In this step, we will make our deadlines for each small task. The purpose of this is so you have a general idea when you have to finish each task. If you don't finish one step by the deadline you have set, you jeopardize every step that you have planned after that. This chain reaction helps create some urgency.

- Step 4: Get Rid Of As Many Temptations As You Can

If you are a constant procrastination offender, it may be because you make it very easy for yourself to be distracted. Be self-aware – what are the things you typically find yourself doing when you're supposed to be doing something else? Is it browsing the internet? Is it scrolling on your phone? Identify what exactly it is that is tempting you to procrastinate and try to prevent yourself from being tempted in the first place. If you are easily distracted by your phone, turn it off for an hour, put it in a drawer, and begin to work. Some people may be extreme and go as far as disabling all their social media accounts to prevent themselves from endless browsing. It doesn't have to be extremely drastic but take preventative measures, so it's not too easy for you to procrastinate.

- Step 5: Be In The Company Of Those Who Inspire You

Choosing who you spend your time with heavily influences your behaviors. If you are spending time with people who procrastinate and don't see anything wrong with it, you are likely to think that that is okay. Instead, try to surround yourself with people that are motivated and have achieved many goals before. You will soon be able to gain some of their motivation and spirit as well.

- Step 6: Find Someone To Hold You Accountable

When you have a large set of tasks that you need to get done, having a buddy will make the process way more fun, your buddy should ideally be someone that also has their own large set of tasks/goals that they want to complete. The two of you will hold each other accountable for the tasks that you need to do. Both of you do not need to have the same goals, but if you do, that's even better! Many people with goals of getting more fit will likely find themselves a workout buddy that will help hold them accountable for going to the gym or even planning workout sessions together.

- Step 7: Share Your Goals With Your Friends And Family

This step serves a similar function as the step before but on a much larger scale. Tell your friends, family, and colleagues about the goals that you have in mind. This step works better if you tell them details like your deadlines or the plan you've made for yourself. The next time you see these people, they will likely ask you what your status is on your goals, creating motivation for you. Also, people tend not to want to 'fail' in front of others, so if you know that you are seeing those people soon, you are more likely to make sure that you have made some progress in updating them on it.

- Step 8: Connect With Someone Who Has Achieved Similar Goals As You

If your goal is one that you think other people have accomplished before, try to find out who these people are. Seek them out and connect with them to ask them about their experience. You can learn about what obstacles and failures they faced along the way, and they'd be able to provide you with some tips that may have made their journey a little bit easier. Moreover, seeing living proof that your goals are achievable ones may help you take action even sooner.

- Step 9: Refresh Your Goals Often

If you are someone that has been procrastinating for a long time now, it might be due to the misalignment of what you're currently doing and what you want. People often outgrow their goals when they begin to learn more about themselves. However, they don't always adjust their goals based on those changes. Try to take a weekend to yourself and regroup. Ask yourself, 'what exactly do I want to achieve? Are the things that I am doing now aligning with that? If not, what can I do to change it?' Adjusting your goals to something that lines up with who you are presently is crucial in creating motivation and value.

- Step 10: Simplify Things As Much As You Can

You may be identifying all the reasons why the present moment is 'not the best time,' but that is the wrong mindset to have. Even if you only had

10 minutes, you can surely get SOMETHING done related to your goal. Abandon this thought of waiting for 'the perfect time' because there will never be one. After you break down your goals into smaller ones, start doing them whenever you have 10 minutes free. It's as simple as that.

• Step 11: Use Your Willpower And Just Do It

At the end of it all, everything comes down to simply just taking action. Just like how we learned motivation comes from starting something and not before, simply taking the first step to doing something will create the motivation you need to keep you going. A person can do all the planning and strategizing they need, but nothing will happen if they don't take the first step.

CHAPTER 6
Building Good Habits

In this chapter, I will provide you with more tips and habits that will help you strengthen your self-discipline even more. If you've ever read any psychology books in the past, you would know that a lot of what a person does every day is very habit driven.

You might even know from your own experience that some people don't like to stray away from their habits and routines. If a person develops the right habits, they can have stronger self-discipline without feeling like they are draining their willpower. People tend to lose self-discipline when they feel like their willpower has been drained, and they can no longer resist the temptations in their lives. For this reason, we will take this chapter to talk about habits and how they can benefit you.

What Are Habits?

Our habits are made up of neural pathways that have been imprinted into our brains. This is something that happens on a biological level. These neural pathways are responsible for linking up the neural networks in a person's brain to perform specific functions without thinking about it. These neural pathways help a person automate certain behaviors that they constantly use to reduce the energy needed for the conscious processing power in a person's brain. Automating certain actions allows this person's mind to focus on other things rather than the mundane tasks they have done a thousand times. This function stems from our very early human days and is a part of our DNA. This function allows us to have a more efficient mind that can be used for many things and not entirely focused on simple daily tasks.

You may know that you don't like straying away from your existing habits and routines from your own experience. It feels uncomfortable. Humans tend to find comfort in old habits and routines. Unfortunately, a lot of the time our habits are not positive ones. Most people tend to have bad habits such as indulging in the conveniences of junk food, drinking alcohol every night, or skipping the gym for an extra hour of sleep. If you have a couple of bad habits yourself, you may know very well that the urge to act out these habits are very strong. However, there is a silver lining to this. If bad habits can be so strong and tempting, good habits can be like that. It all comes down to a matter of incorporating those good habits in your life and ingraining it so deeply that it feels wrong or uncomfortable not to act out those habits.

It is often the mundane behaviors that we repeat most, making them our most ingrained habit. These habits that are ingrained hold people back from building good habits. Most of the time, people tend to have more bad habits that add negative value to their lives rather than good habits that further help them reach their goals. Since neural pathways get ingrained deeper and deeper over time, it is difficult for people to break out of their bad habits or form good ones when they are constantly acting out on bad habits.

The Importance of Habits

When we are children, we learn habits and make associations without knowing it that we often carry into our later lives. While this is no fault of yours, recognizing it as a potential issue is important to make changes in your adult life. Bad habits are built through many years, and no amount of willpower can handle overcoming that many bad habits in a person's life. Rewiring your brain to minimize the amount of negativity you feel in the first place is a much more efficient method to approach this problem.

To strengthen self-discipline, you need to instill a new habit, which can feel very intimidating at first, especially if you are focusing on the entire goal all at once. To avoid this daunting feeling, keep it very simple. Break your bigger goal into smaller doable ones. As we discussed, instead of trying to accomplish one huge goal all at once or to change all of your habits all at once, focus on doing just one thing consistently and exercise your self-discipline with that one small thing.

For example, if you are looking to get into better shape, start by exercising for 10 to 15 minutes per day. Instead of trying to go to the gym for 2 hours every day, which can be very daunting, start with a smaller goal in mind first. By taking baby steps, you can get your mind used to that habit and slowly increase the amount of time you spend at the gym. Eventually, once you feel like that goal has become a habit, you can then begin to focus on other small goals and keep building up words from there.

Good Habits Versus Bad Habits

Where do habits come from, and how are they developed? Why is it that when many people try to change their habits by breaking the bad ones or building good ones, they only stick with it for a certain amount of time before giving up and going back to their old ways?

The biggest problem here, especially with habits that people have had for many years or even decades, are the neural pathways that have been imprinted into people's brains. This happens on a biological level. These neural pathways are responsible for linking up the neural networks in a person's brain to perform a specific function like preparing a coffee cup in a certain way, walking up the stairs, or smoking a cigarette.

These neural pathways help a person automate behavior that they constantly use as a means of reducing the energy needed for a person's brain's conscious processing power. Doing this allows a person's mind to focus on other things rather than the habitual tasks they have done a thousand times. This function stems from our early days as humans, and it is part of our DNA; it allows humans to have a more efficient mind that they can use for other things rather than mundane things.

However, if you can try to ingrain the next following habits we will be discussing into your life, you will find that strengthening your self-discipline may become easier. Again, these things don't happen overnight. Remember that habits take lots of time to form and even to break. If you start small and take baby steps and build, you will stop thinking about how much longer you can discipline yourself since you will have ingrained those habits into your brain, which automatically promotes the self-discipline you seek.

Good Habits to Build That Will Help You to Increase Your Self-Discipline

In this section, we will look at several habits that you should begin developing to increase your level of self-discipline. You may be asking yourself how some of these habits are related to self-discipline. The answer is this; by living a well-rounded and healthy life, you can exercise your self-discipline, motivation, and willpower when it counts the most. Without further ado, we are going to begin by discussing the first habit- Gratitude.

Habit #1: Gratitude

Gratitude is an important action in human life that helps people with self-discipline and is often used to help people who are facing self-esteem and self-confidence issues. A huge problem in our modern world today is that we are constantly presented with millions of worldly things that cause us always to be wanting something more or something else. This bombardment causes people to spend too much time thinking about all the things they want and not thinking about the things they already have. Building a habit of gratitude helps people move away from constantly wanting the things they don't have and move forward towards appreciating the things they do have. When people do this, they can begin to make remarkable changes in their lives.

The effects of practicing and showcasing gratitude are extremely crucial. It does everything from improving mental health, emotional well-being, a person's spirituality, gratitude is capable of so many things. Practicing gratitude is an exercise that is constantly used in therapy to help the client move away from thinking about things that aren't present and focus on being mindful. Most importantly, gratitude helps people move away towards a state of abundance and away from lack. When people live in a state of lack, they can't focus on achieving their goals and being self-disciplined. They spend too much of their mental energy and capacity worrying about the things they don't have or living fearfully, to the point that they forget about the things they do have.

The state of lack can also show up in someone as physical symptoms. This state produces a lot of stress because the brain automatically releases cortisol and epinephrine, which are the stress hormones from our brains. These hormones impact numerous systems within the human body. When someone is stressed, their immune systems, digestive systems, and reproductive systems are all affected. We must spend a few minutes every day writing down all the things that we are grateful for. Even if you feel like you don't have anything to be grateful for, try hard to find something. It doesn't have to be anything large, like winning the lottery or finding $20 on the ground. It could be something very simple like the nice weather, the nice conversation you had with your barista, or even just seeing a cute dog on your way home.

Habit #2: Forgiveness

If you live a fast-paced life, how often do you find yourself feeling angry, frustrated, or annoyed? Due to the insane amount of convenience we have access to in our daily lives, simple annoyances can cause a spiral of negative emotions in a person's day. For example, if you are in a hurry to get to work and you happen to be running late that day, the coffee shop that you normally stop to get your morning coffee is taking forever to make your order. When you finally get your coffee, you realize that they had made your order wrong, but now you have no time to get it fixed. That one simple human error has spent you into a spiral of anger and annoyance, and you struggle to let go of it, and you find that it is still negatively impacting your whole day. This spiral causes you to have spent most of your energy upset about the coffee shop that wronged you, and you don't have enough mental capacity to focus on other things like practicing your self-discipline. When people spend most of their days feeling the emotions of anger, regret, or guilt, they create more problems than they are with solutions. The emotions of anger and hate consume much more energy in a person's body than positive emotions like forgiveness and love. Forgiveness is something that we can learn. When people learn to forgive, only then will they be able to let go of certain things.

Without learning the habit of forgiveness, people would simply not be able to achieve self-discipline. When a person is too worried about how someone or something has wronged them, it makes it impossible for them to focus on achieving their goals or on their discipline. If someone has hurt you in the past, learn to forgive them. It doesn't mean that you have to forget about what they did to you altogether. Simply just forgive and let go of that negative energy and give it back to the universe rather than keeping it within your body. When we perform the act of forgiveness, we are letting go of the negative energy that inhibits our ability to practice self-discipline. If you want to master self-discipline, you have to get rid of sources that are sucking away at your mental energy. Holding on to negative emotions like anger is a sure way for you to drain your energy. While forgiveness might not seem like a discipline habit when you first look at it, it is an extremely crucial one to build in the process.

Try to think about the people or situations that you are currently angry with. It could be someone you think has wronged you recently, or simply just an annoying situation that has happened to you. Instead of just thinking about how it made you feel, try to put yourself in their shoes. What would be the things that you would do if you were in their situation? Make it light-hearted and try to find some humor in it. Rather than thinking about it as a situation that shouldn't have happened, try to find a lesson learned in those situations. I know that it is very hard to forgive certain people, especially if they have hurt you or wronged you in life. However, it isn't until people can let go of those feelings of hatred and hurt before things in their life begin to improve. People are often so busy stressing and worrying that they don't spend enough time thinking about how they will change their future.

Habit #3: Meditation

Just like gratitude, meditation is a commonly used technique to help people practice mindfulness when they are suffering from an anxiety disorder or depression disorder. Meditation is something that you can use to help put your mind at ease. It can also provide you with a spiritual centeredness that can be used as an avenue of growth. When people meditate, they take their awareness away from things of the past and the future and focus it on the present. When this happens, they can connect themselves to the universe, which also increases gratitude.

In the later chapters of this book, we will learn how meditation can help a person improve their self-discipline. Meditation plays a big role in a person's ability to use their willpower. Its function is to clear the mind of any thoughts and simply focus all attention on the present. From a self-discipline perspective, meditation helps set the right tone for a person's day. Also, it helps people improve their physical, emotional, and mental health all at once, allowing them to gain some of the biggest benefits for the least amount of time invested.

There are many types of meditation, some of which focus on mindfulness, focusing on love and gratitude. There truly are too many different types of meditation for humankind to keep track of. The most popular and beneficial type used amongst many therapies and within self-discipline is mindfulness meditation. Contrary to common belief, meditation doesn't have to take a long time. It can be done in 10 to 15 minutes. However, the hardest part of meditation is bringing yourself to do it. A person has to keep their mind still and train it to stop wandering all the time. The trick behind mindfulness meditation is not to stop wandering thoughts altogether, but simply to acknowledge these thoughts and reroute yourself back to the present. There are many types of breathing techniques that can be accompanied with meditation to help with achieving mindfulness. We will be diving deeper into these techniques in the meditation chapter.

Some people believe that meditation is about aligning the physical human body with its spiritual body. However, for this book, we will stay away from spirituality and focus more on the practical benefit of being mindful.

Habit #4: Active Goal Setting

We have mentioned this briefly in the previous chapter, but it is important enough that we will mention it again. In the previous chapter, we learned that setting attainable goals is more effective than setting Broad and large goals. Setting smaller goals becomes more quantifiable, and because of this, you can easily keep track of how you are doing when it comes to goal achievement.

Active goal setting is very different from passive goal-setting. Passive goal setting means you are setting goals in your mind, and they are passive because they lack many details. Passive goal-setting means that a person hasn't properly defined the actual goal, making it hard for them to keep track of their progress and know what needs they must do to achieve that goal. Active goal setting is the complete opposite of passive goal-setting. Active goal setting means writing out these goals and making sure that they have an important meeting. These goals have to be measurable and very specific. To successfully have an active goal, a person has to make a plan towards achieving it. This plan is why people set long-term goals and engage in smaller goals daily to achieve a bigger goal.

Using active goal-setting ingrains the discipline in us because it forces us to give ourselves a direction. By breaking down your big goals into smaller daily goals, it helps people avoid distractions by only looking at what they need to get done in the present day. This way, a person isn't left constantly thinking about one large intimidating goal but not knowing how to approach it.

Active goal setting works by taking the first step in setting your long-term goals. Suppose you have long-term goals like; wanting to own your first home, wanting to pay off your student debt by the next three years, or taking six months off to travel Europe. If you have long-term goals, you need to actively participate in daily, weekly, and monthly goal setting and planning. You have to play an active role in tracking your progress towards your goals and making changes in places where you feel like you aren't working.

So take out a pen and a piece of paper, and start writing down what long-term goals you have. Once you have some long-term goals written down, break it down into monthly, weekly, and daily goals. Start slowly by accomplishing your daily goals, and when you reach the end of the month, assess to see if you have achieved your monthly goal through accomplishing your daily goals. If you haven't, look back on your daily goals and see if there's anything you can change to achieve next month's goal.

Habit #5: Eat Healthily

We also discussed the benefits of eating healthy in the previous chapter, but we will expand on it slightly more here. Many people don't realize that our human body spends a huge portion of its energy digesting and processing food. When a person's diet is rich in proteins, fats, and carbohydrates, their body uses more energy to process food, which some of it is useless to us.

Raw fruits and foods offer the biggest boost of energy for humans because they require less energy to process and provide more energy for the body to use after that. This process is called an enhanced Thermic Effect of Food (TEF) or known as Dietary Induced Thermogenesis (DIT).

As we learned in the previous chapter, our brains use up a large amount of glucose to keep functioning. Therefore, the amount of energy that a person has is very responsible and how focused they feel. When a person is focussed, they can achieve their goals using less willpower than if they weren't focused. When a person feels too comatose from the unhealthy food they have eaten, staying focused is very hard to achieve. They often spend too much of their time feeling too sluggish and tired to work on achieving their goals.

You commonly hear that breakfast is the most important meal of the day. However, it's important not only to eat a healthy breakfast but to eat multiple healthy meals throughout the day. To do this, you have to actively plan what you're going to eat during these meals to break some of your bad habits. For example, if you plan to eat five healthy smaller-sized meals per day, but you haven't prepared any of those meals, you are more likely to feel hungry and indulge in unhealthy conveniences like fast food. If you are someone who eats fast food or processed foods often, your body won't create enough energy to help you approach your goals with focus or help you have the willpower to start working at them.

Since the food that a person eats can change their brain's neural chemical makeup, it also heavily influences a person's mind and body connection. Take a look at the things that you eat during your day. Try to find the meals where you often indulge in unhealthy food or junk food. Plan so you can substitute those meals with raw, organic, and healthy foods. By buying this type of healthy food in advance and preparing it for the times you become hungry, you will be less likely to visit your nearest McDonalds.

Habit #6: Sleep

Since the theory behind willpower is that it gets its energy from the brain, which gets its energy from glucose levels and rest, it's safe to assume that sleep is directly connected to how the brain can acquire energy. When a person doesn't get enough sleep, their brain spends most of its energy focused on just keeping your basic body functions up and going. This expenditure does not leave much energy for a person to spend on exerting their willpower, practicing self-discipline, or simply remembering their self-discipline. Getting the proper and healthy amount of sleep is a vital requirement for accomplishing anything. When a person doesn't get enough sleep, it affects their ability to focus, their judgment, mood, overall health, and diet.

When people suffer chronic sleep deprivation, such as insomnia, things go from bad to worse. Many research studies have found evidence that people who don't get the proper amount of sleep regularly have a greater risk of catching specific diseases. Lack of sleep also has a significant and negative impact on a person's immune system. This lack of sleep can cause a person to frequently catch colds or touches of flu that cause them not to go to school, work, or get anything done effectively.

For an adult, it is important to get at least six hours of sleep every night. A healthy amount of sleep should range between eight to ten hours every night, but the minimum amount is 6 hours. Avoid eating or drinking anything that contains caffeine at least 5 hours before bedtime so that it doesn't affect your natural sleep cycle. Make a note to avoid ingesting too many toxins during the day, such as cigarettes, alcohol, drugs, or prescription medicine, if you can avoid it.

In conclusion, the benefits of getting enough sleep are extraordinary. Aside from the fact that it can help you stay focused and be more disciplined, it also helps you curb inflammation and pain, lower stress, improves your memory, jumpstart your creativity, sharpens your attention, improves your grades, limits your chances for accidents, and helps you avoid depression.

Habit #7: Exercise

Exercise is one of the most important habits to build within all people. It acts as a cornerstone habit to help a person's life be filled with positive habits and get rid of the bad ones. A person who can discipline themselves has to instill the habit of exercise into their everyday routine. As you all may already know, there are endless benefits when it comes to exercise. The benefits of exercise are talked about not only by psychologists but medical experts as well. Even though exercise is such an important component of a person's life, not everyone prioritizes it. Why is this?

In our busy modern-day lives, everyone gets caught up trying to get all the things that they need to get done and are often busy running around completing errands and failing to tackle exercise head-on simply. Often, people have a bad mindset when it comes to exercise and think that they won't build it as a habit because they simply have "too many other things to do." This thought process is where most people are wrong. There are ways to incorporate exercise even if their day is jam-packed from beginning to end.

When people think of exercise, they may automatically think of a minimum one-hour intense weight-lifting session at the gym, a one-hour long, expensive spin class, or a one-hour yoga class. If that's what they are thinking about, then yes, indeed, the people that have busy lives may not be able to incorporate the time to get to their exercise class, the time it takes to complete the exercise class, and then get to wherever they need to go after that. However, exercise doesn't necessarily have to be a formalized session that takes a long time. It can simply be getting some sit-ups, push-ups, or some jumping jacks in the morning before you head to work. It can also be you choosing to walk to work instead of taking the bus, or it could be a brief walk around your neighborhood park after dinner.

Instilling exercise as a keystone habit of your life can help you become more disciplined and improve your life in numerous ways. First of all, exercise effectively reduces stress levels and pain because it causes the brain to release feel-good endorphins and neurotransmitters like serotonin and dopamine. Secondly, exercise helps increase the oxygenation and blood flow of body cells, which helps boost the immune system and fight off diseases. Lastly, exercise increases a person's ability to focus on the task at hand due to the increased activity in the brain, which allows us to live a more disciplined life.

So start building the habit of exercise in your life by simply just going for a 10-minute walk or just doing some sit-ups and push-ups right after you wake up. Just a few minutes is fine. Try to do this for one week and then increase the amount of time you spend on that session next week. Keep up with this pattern, and soon enough, you will have a healthy amount of time every day that you set aside to get your exercise in, and this is when it will become a full-blown habit.

Habit #8: Organization

Have you ever noticed that when your home is messy, it makes it very hard to be comfortable and therefore leads you to be unfocused and distracted? Naturally, humans don't like living in a dirty and messy environment. For a person to achieve their goals and accomplish self-discipline, they need to get organized. The organization also needs to become a fully incorporated habit into a person's personal life and professional life. This organization includes the physical act of organizing the things you have in your home and the mental act of organizing the things on your mind.

By living an organized life, you are living a disciplined life. If you are someone who is constantly scattered and disorganized, start small with your organization skills. Just pick one small space each day for yourself to organize. This act can be just one single drawer in your kitchen, the things lying around on your desk, or just straighten out the things on your coffee table. The next day, pick something else to organize like your bathroom drawers or the clothes in your closet. The more time you spend living in a clean and organized environment, the less you would want your home to become cluttered and messy again. You will begin to notice when clutter builds up, and by having a habit of organization, you will immediately organize things as you use them, so you don't have to spend time organizing it later on.

By decluttering your home or your working environment, you will have plenty of different areas where you can sit down and work on your own goals. Has your home ever been so cluttered that when you do have the motivation to start working on something, you simply don't have the space to do it? To avoid this, keep your home clean and organized at all times so that when you have a rush of motivation, you can find a workspace that is clean and ready for you to work.

Like many other habits, the habit of an organization can be learned and built over time. It requires your attention and effort, but it will pay off tremendously in the long run. When you live in a physical space that is organized and clean, your mind will automatically become more stress-free, relaxed, and give you the ability to focus. In turn, by becoming more organized, you are increasing your ability to be more self-disciplined. Begin to incorporate this good habit of putting things back where it belongs when you're finished using it rather than leaving it out. Little things like this we do daily have the largest impact on the quality of life. Pay attention to small things, and you'll begin to see big benefits.

Habit #9: Time Management

In the busy world that we live in today, time management is extremely crucial if you are trying to get everything that you need to get done. An average person has to work 40 hours a week, not including the time it takes for them to commute to work, and still have to make time for things like exercise, relationships, socializing, family, and achieving the goals they have set. Without good time management, it will be virtually impossible for anyone to get anything done unless they can manage their time effectively.

When people can properly manage their time, they will begin to have room to do the things that matter. Mainly, they must make room to do the activities that they need to achieve the goals that they have set. To achieve their long-term goals, they have to break it down into smaller daily goals that may not be the most urgent but are still very important. If a person does not have good time management, they likely cannot even get the most urgent things they need to get done in a day, let alone achieve goals that don't require immediate urgency.

To effectively measure if certain things are urgent, non-urgent, important, not important, you need to take a second to think about whether or not the action that you are doing is not 'urgent but important' or 'not urgent and not important' or 'urgent and important.' The things that fall into the 'not urgent and not important' category are known as things that are time-wasters. This category includes things like browsing social media on your phone or binge-watching your favorite Netflix series. Things that fall into the category of 'not urgent but important' are likely the short-term goals you have set for yourself. Although you don't need to complete them urgently, they are still important for your self-growth. Things that are urgent and important are likely deadlines or any responsibilities that you have to complete for your work.

A person's ability to strengthen self-discipline comes from their ability to manage their time. Some of the most successful people in the world are incredible time managers because, rather than using time as a detractor, they use the time to benefit. Everybody has the same amount of time in a day; we shouldn't waste it. Start managing your time by categorizing what you need to do in a day with the categories I gave you above. Start by doing the urgent and important things, then move on to the things that are non-urgent but important. Leave the things that are both not urgent or important until the end of the day when you have completed all the other things. This way, you are maximizing your time to get the things that you need to get completed.

Habit #10: Persistence

This last habit you probably saw coming. No amount of self-discipline would ever be complete without the presence of persistence. Persistence is a habit that helps us not give up, even when we face failure head-on. Persistence helps us get back up on our feet to keep trying even when we do fail. Persistence plays such a huge role in self-discipline that without it, achieving self-discipline is probably impossible.

You might be wondering why that is. The reason for this is because achieving our goals is not an easy thing to do. It is really hard. Getting discouraged is easy and something that happens to everyone along their journey. Also, giving up takes far less energy and effort than continuing to push through even if it's something that causes a lot of pain in the process before it can give us any pleasure.

However, this hardship required to achieve any goals is simply something that you have to persevere through because that's just what it takes. We all have to realize that even the most successful people in the world have failed numerous times over and over again. Failure is simply a part of life, and rather than avoiding it and not pursuing your goals at all in fear of failure, we should learn to persevere and push through even during the hardest of times. Without fail, we wouldn't achieve the big goals that we have set for ourselves.

There are many ways that a person can go about instilling perseverance as a habit, but the best and most effective weight is to develop the reasons you want to do the things in life that you aim for. If the reasons behind your goals are strong enough, they can motivate you so you can get through anything.

CHAPTER 7
Increasing Your Self-Discipline

In this chapter, we will focus on learning some of the challenges that come with strengthening your self-discipline. We already know that hardship and failure are a part of the process of life and building self-discipline. Understanding what these challenges might be in advance gives you an idea of what to prepare for when faced with an obstacle. Like we mentioned earlier in this book, having a plan prepared when you are in the face of a challenge or temptation can help you react in a good way rather than in a way that negatively affects your progress.

Steps to Achieving a Higher Level of Self-Discipline

The best way to not fall into temptations while using your self-discipline is to avoid temptation in the first place. Figuring out your weaknesses and temptations is crucial in maintaining self-discipline, as we have mentioned numerous times throughout the book.

You can do things to learn self-discipline and tap into your will power source to live a happier life. Below are ten steps that you should follow to master your self-discipline over ten days.

- Step 1: Learn what your weaknesses are.

Everyone has their own set of weaknesses. They could range from a certain type of food like chocolate, or it can be social media like Instagram, or even the latest addictive video game. Regardless of what it is, it has a similar effect on everyone.

The first step to mastering your self-discipline is acknowledging your shortcomings, no matter what they might be. People often try to pretend that their weaknesses don't exist to portray themselves as a strong person. This portrayal is extremely ineffective when it comes to self-discipline. The purpose of acknowledging your weaknesses is not to make yourself feel bad; instead, it helps you recognize what they are and help you plan to overcome them. Acknowledge your flaws; it is impossible to overcome them until you do this.

- Step 2: Remove all your temptations.

Once you have acknowledged your weaknesses, you can now move on to step two, remove your temptations. Like we mentioned in step one, everyone has their own set of weaknesses, and it can range from small things like an unhealthy snack to something that hinders your productivity, like playing a video game for hours on end. By understanding your weaknesses, you can make accommodations for yourself that will help remove some of those temptations.

For example, if somebody is looking to lose weight and get fit at the gym, but they know that their weakness is that they always eat chocolate after dinner every night. In this case, their temptation removal would be not to buy any more chocolate that they keep around in their home. By not having chocolate in the home, they would be unable to fall into the temptation of eating it, which will hinder their progress of getting fit. However, this does not mean that they will never be able to eat chocolate again. This change only means that they can indulge in their favorite snacks when they have achieved a certain portion of their goal. Rewarding oneself is important to self-discipline, as well.

- Step 3: Set the defined goals and create an execution plan.

To continue strengthening your self-discipline, a person must have a clear vision of what goals they are trying to accomplish. They must also have an understanding of what success means to them. If a person doesn't know where they're planning to go or what accomplishing their goals even and Tails, it is easy for them to lose their way or get sidetracked.

Make sure the goals that you are setting have a clear and concise purpose. For example, don't use goals like "I want to be rich by the next five years." This goal is too broad for it to have a strong meaning. Instead, you should make a goal that is quantifiable like "I am planning on saving $20,000 by the end of this year". Then, when you have a quantifiable goal, you can make a plan that makes sense for yourself. In this example, a person can plan to save $2,000 each month for the rest of this year to hit their goal of saving $20,000 by the end of it. They can break down these goals even further and figure out where they can save money or how they can make more money to accomplish that goal in their budget.

- Step 4: Begin Building your self-discipline.

Self-discipline is not something that people are born with; it is mostly a learned behavior. Self-discipline is just like any other skill that people may be looking to grow; it requires repetition and daily practice. Like going to the gym, the more you work out your muscles, the bigger and stronger they will become. Changes do not happen overnight; instead, to strengthen your muscles and grow them, it will take at least several weeks for a person to see their progress. The effort and focus that training self-discipline requires can be extremely tiring.

The more time you practice self-discipline, the more it can become difficult to keep utilizing your willpower. Sometimes when a person faces a big temptation or decision, they may feel that overcoming that large temptation makes it harder for them to overcome other tasks requiring self-discipline. The only way to move past this is to have a good mindset. By having a good mindset, it creates a buffer for how quickly your willpower becomes drained. Also, like the muscle example we used, by exerting your willpower more often, you will have a higher tolerance and therefore be able to exert it more than if you were just starting.

- Step 5: Keep it simple and create new habits.

To strengthen self-discipline, you need to instill a new habit, which can feel very intimidating at first, especially if you are focusing on the entire goal all at once. To avoid this daunting feeling, keep it very simple. Break your bigger goal into smaller doable ones. Instead of trying to accomplish one huge goal all at once or to change all of your habits, focus on doing just one thing consistently, and exercise your self-discipline with that one small thing.

For example, if you are looking to get into better shape, start by exercising for 10 to 15 minutes per day. Instead of trying to go to the gym for 2 hours every day, which can be very daunting, start with a smaller goal in mind first. By taking baby steps, you can get your mind used to that habit and slowly increase the amount of time you spend at the gym. Eventually, once you feel like that goal has become a habit, you can then begin to focus on other small goals and keep building up words from there.

- Step 6: Implement a healthier diet.

In the earlier chapters, we learned that glucose levels play a big role in a person's brain power, which controls a person's willpower. The sensation of being hungry can cause people to feel angry, annoyed, and irritated. This feeling is real, and everyone has felt it before, and often has a huge impact on a person's willpower. Research has found evidence that having low blood sugar weakens a person's ability to make good decisions.

When a person is hungry, their ability to concentrate suffers a lot, and their brains don't function optimally. Therefore, a person's self-control is likely to be weakened when their body is in this state. To prevent this, make sure to be eating small meals constantly to prevent yourself from feeling that annoying hungry feeling that causes people to have a lapse in judgment. Since exercising willpower takes up a lot of energy from a person's brain, make sure to keep fuelling it with enough glucose so that the brain can keep functioning at an optimal level.

- Step 7: Adjust your views regarding willpower.

In the earlier chapters, we learned that a person's point of view or their beliefs could create a buffer of how long it takes to have their willpower drained completely. Although most researchers believe that there is a limit to how much we can tap into our willpower, they also found that the people who believe that there wasn't a limit had a bigger will power stockpile. If a person believes that they have a limited amount of willpower, they probably will not surpass those limits. However, if a person does not place a strict limit on themselves, they are less likely to use up their willpower stockpile before meeting their goals.

A person's internal perception about their willpower and self-control plays a huge role in determining how much willpower they have. If a person can remove these obstacles by believing that they have a large stockpile of willpower and believing in themselves, they are less likely to drain out their willpower than someone who believes that they don't have

much of it. So try changing your perception of how you see your willpower. Try to think of it as a source that can run out, but you have a larger amount of it because of your beliefs. This mindset is a much better mindset than thinking that willpower will run out, so you should be stingy with it.
- Step 8: Make a backup plan.

Many psychologists use a famous technique that helps with boosting willpower called "implementation intention." This technique is where you give yourself a plan when you face a potentially difficult situation. We used this example earlier; if a person is trying to reduce the amount of alcohol that they drink and they know that they are going to a party where they will be asked if they want to drink alcohol, instead of always asking for a beer like they normally do, they will instead ask for a plain soda with lime.

By making a plan before going to a situation where you know where you will face big temptations, you will have an action plan where you can automatically use rather than have to come up with an excuse on the spot and risking failure. When a person goes into those situations with a plan, it helps give them the mindset and self-control necessary to overcome obstacles. They will save energy by not having to make sudden decisions or make sudden plans based on their emotional state. This practice will make them less likely to cave into temptations and more likely to exercise their self-discipline.
- Step 9: Reward yourself.

Like anything else in life, it is necessary to give yourself a break and reward yourself. Give yourself something to look forward to by planning an appropriate reward when you accomplish your goals. This reward system is not much different from when you were a little kid, and you got a treat from your parents for showing good behavior. When a person has something to look forward to, it gives them the extra motivation to succeed.

Anticipation is a powerful thing. It gives people something to focus on so that they are not only thinking of all the things they need to change. When you have achieved one of your goals, you can find yourself a new goal and a new reward to keep motivating yourself to move forward. However, the reward should not be something unhealthy. For example, in the previous example of the person trying to lower their alcohol intake, their reward for not drinking as often should not be that they will go binge drinking next Friday. Their awards should be something healthy that won't make them lose progress on all the work that they've done.
- Step 10: Keep moving forward using forgiveness.

Even if a person has all the best intentions and the most well-made plans, sometimes they will fall short when practicing self-discipline. Avoiding failure altogether is impossible, and we should not build a mindset around that. Everyone will have their ups and downs, their successes, and their failures. The key to overcoming the failures that you will face is simply to keep moving forward. If you stumble on your journey of self-discipline, instead of giving up altogether, acknowledge what caused it, learn from it, and then move on. Don't let yourself get caught up in frustration, anger, or guilt because these emotions are the ones that will de-motivate you and get in the way of your future progress. Learn from the mistakes you have made and be comfortable with forgiving yourself. Once you have done that, you can get your head back in the game and start where you left off.

How to Overcome Obstacles

Your mindset plays a huge role in your success when it comes to change. The way you view your journey will make or break it and determine whether or not your change is lasting or fleeting and whether or not you become invested in making the changes in your life.

One problem that people normally face when trying to strengthen their self-discipline is falling into a self-defeating loop. It looks like this:

Fail to engage in desired behavior > negative/physical/psychological consequences > low mood, shame, and self-criticism > low motivation to engage in healthy behaviors.

This loop continues in a positive feedback loop that is very difficult to get yourself out of.

Even if a person has all the best intentions and the most well-made plans, sometimes they will fall short when practicing self-discipline. Avoiding failure altogether is impossible, and we should not build a mindset around that. Everyone will have their ups and downs, their successes, and their failures. The key to overcoming the failures that you will face is simply to keep moving forward. If you stumble on your journey of self-discipline, instead of giving up altogether, acknowledge what caused it, learn from it, and then move on. Don't let yourself get caught up in frustration, anger, or guilt because these emotions are the ones that will de-motivate you and get in the way of your future progress. Learn from the mistakes you have made and be comfortable with forgiving yourself. Once you have done that, you can get your head back in the game and start where you left off.

Challenges to Anticipate

In this chapter, we will look at several challenges that you should anticipate as you work on increasing your level of self-discipline. By foreseeing these obstacles, you can feel prepared, rather than feeling surprised when they come about. Before you begin, take some time to write in your journal about what some possible obstacles may be. Once you have done this, take some time to plan and decide how you will deal with them when they arise, so that they do not disrupt your progress or cause you to resort to old ways that are unhealthy.

By setting yourself up for success in this way, you will be able to tackle any challenge without having your new lifestyle jeopardized. Below you can see the most common challenges and obstacles that you may face on this journey.

Fighting Against 'Natural' Tendencies

People often feel like their natural state should be sitting on their couch, with a plethora of snacks, and watching their favorite TV show. During those days, the idea of going to the gym or even just eating a healthy meal seems to be absurd. Interestingly, people nowadays have been conditioned by society's expectations to think that their natural state is lazy. If you are not constantly on-the-go or working your butt off at work, we live in a world where you are not working hard enough. The result of these feelings is that people tend to get trapped, thinking that practicing self-discipline is the constant battle of fighting against a person's natural state. Their mindset is one that is a psychological battle of laziness versus self-discipline. Having this type of mindset makes it difficult to practice self-discipline.

One of the reasons that I suspect behind this mindset is that people tend to mistake the need for rest to be lazy. Lots of mental or physical exertion creates fatigue in the human body. Rest is a recovery process so that the person can get stronger and be able to repeat and exceed that mental and physical exertion. If your mindset regarding self-discipline is constant and uninterrupted, you deny your body's natural need for recovery and rest. This need for recovery will show itself as sabotage of your self-discipline efforts, and you will automatically label it as lazy. Be careful when this happens, as this label is very incorrect.

Rather than mistaking any urges of rest as a sign of being lazy, think about whether or not you have exerted yourself already. If so, it is all right to stop what you're doing and take a quick break to recharge. Getting into the mindset that you are lazy or that resting is for lazy people, you will always feel negative about yourself every time your body shows you a natural symptom when asking you to rest.

The World Doesn't Care About Your Attempts at Self-Discipline.

When a person decides to actively and purposefully restructure their life and behavior, the universe doesn't just magically make things easier for them. On the contrary, it will likely throw many challenges at you. It may rain the day that you decide to go out for a run, or your coworker might buy you a whole box of chocolates just to be nice on the day that you decide to eat healthily.

Since the world isn't built on fairness or justice or reward, it is silly to think that the universe will consciously support the changes that you are trying to make in your life. Some people claim that the universe presents opportunities to them when they have decided to change their lives. This thought is inaccurate because if a person is looking to change their life, they likely have taken on new activities. By being exposed to new people and new information, this creates new opportunities that have nothing to do with the universe trying to help you. So don't spend time thinking about whether or not your self-discipline plan is something that the universe will help you with. Spend your time instead of preparing for all the obstacles that will get in your way of achieving your goals. If you do run into obstacles, which you will, don't think that they are there deliberately to throw you off, but they were already there in the first place.

Difficulty Breaking Well-Worn Emotional Behavior Pathways

One of the most well-known concepts in Psychology is that people's emotions are very powerful influences on their behavior. These emotions and feelings are developed throughout human evolution to help us with survival. Negative emotions that people often feel, like fear and anxiety, lets them know that danger is nearby. Feelings of happiness or excitability tell us it's okay to approach the situation. The feeling of anger lets us know that it may be an opportunity where we would need to fight. Sadness lets us know when we need to seek comfort from our loved ones. However, as people, we have learned that emotions and feelings aren't always the best guide to how we behave. People may get anxious in situations that don't have any real danger or get angry in situations where fighting isn't an appropriate reaction. Throughout our lives, we've learned to pick up different habits of ways to react when it comes to responding and managing our emotions. For example, if someone had a rough day after work, their habitual behavior would be to drink a couple of glasses of wine. They do this because this action has worked for them in the past, but they may not realize that they need to change it when they may have outgrown his habit. Some people may try to numb their feelings of sadness or stress by scrolling on their phones to prevent themselves from thinking about other things.

These emotional habits come from the roots of somebody's childhood, where they first learned how to deal with their emotions. Without knowing, people may learn that numbing their emotions is the best strategy for not dealing with the negative ones, or they may try to distract themselves with unhealthy things like alcohol or food. These strategies become reinforced when a person repeatedly uses them and has received success in the past from it. By the time children become adults, they have built some emotion to behavior pathways that are not very well-established and hard to break. This kind of habit is why people have so much trouble strengthening their self-discipline because habits that have formed over the decades require lots of time and willpower to break down and rebuild new ones.

In establishing new habits, it also means that people will have to confront their well-worn habit. For example, if a person's goal was to eat healthily and get in shape, they may have to face their habit of comforting themselves with food and abandon it altogether. Although it may not seem like this is an emotional event, people subconsciously grow very attached to their coping mechanisms. By giving that up altogether, people often feel like they are stripped of their safety net. This feeling means that strengthening and practicing self-discipline is very hard and emotional work. People have managed the emotions and feelings through using their coping mechanisms now become very apparent to them because the coping mechanism was removed. This removal typically doesn't make people very happy, and they often have trouble dealing with their emotions without the safety net that they would always fall back on. By understanding this important concept, you can prepare yourself for the difficulties you will face when practicing your self-discipline. Some of the practices and work that you put in will be very emotionally challenging. You may be able to initiate changes in your life using some simple and concrete goals that you've made for yourself, but you may quickly learn that you would have to face them head-on along your journey if there is emotional baggage.

Being Self-Disciplined Does Not Make You a Popular Person

When people first begin practicing self-discipline and are excited to make good changes in their lives, they often hope that their efforts will inspire other people to get into good habits. They think that by changing into a better person and achieving the goals they've always wanted to achieve for themselves, they will respect other people. This thought process is normal because why wouldn't you want to share with your loved ones that you are changing your life for the better?

However, in reality, most people will just think that the person trying to change is annoying because they go from being easy-going about what they eat to having major food restrictions if they are trying to change their diet. They will begin saying no to certain activities that get in the way of them achieving their goals. They will prioritize other important things regarding the goals that they are going after rather than spending time with people that may not be exactly beneficial to them. Being self-disciplined is not something that is going to make a person more likable.

To be a socially desirable person, you have to be willing to spend a lot of your time with other people doing things that are often unhealthy, like eating out and drinking socially. Let's say that this person manages to strike a really good balance between achieving their goals and remaining socially desirable. Any success that they achieve isn't necessarily going to inspire others. This is because of two reasons. The first reason is that people won't care because they have their problems to deal with most of the time. The second reason is that watching someone else have success when it comes to achieving goals while they're struggling with their own goals is not always inspirational; they may even see it as annoying. People may even consciously or unconsciously attempt to throw you off track because they can't bear to look at their own lives due to jealousy or other emotions.

Just to clarify, other people may not be trying to throw you off track maliciously. I don't think that people would intentionally want you to fail. However, I do think that your attempts at practicing self-discipline to take control of your own life is not something that gets you admiration and respect from other people. Relationships are very complex interactions, and sometimes doing healthier things in life gets you more respect and admiration than living a healthy life. The message I'm trying to get across here is that self-discipline should be something that you pursue yourself and your intrinsic reasons. You should not be doing it to seek congratulation or respect from others because you will likely get the opposite.

Motivation and Inspiration May Be Absent

Some people may have multiple goals that they are looking to achieve. For example, it could be a mix of getting more exercise, eating healthier, pursuing a musical instrument, and being successful in their career. However, it may be that not all of those things can create inspiration or motivation. Out of those goals, there may only be one item that produces the most inspiration and motivation for a person.

Somewhere along the way of self-discipline, a lot of people realize that motivation and inspiration precede action. With this belief comes the expectation that the presence of inspiration and motivation will tell people what they need to do with their lives. They think that wherever there is motivation and inspiration, that is the direction that they should be heading. Although this is a lovely notion, it is not one that lines up with reality. Take someone's university degree as an example. I can almost guarantee that many days when a person doesn't feel inspired or motivated to do their schoolwork. Still, it doesn't change the reality that having a university degree is a very beneficial addition to your life. If a person were to be using motivation and inspiration as a guide, that degree likely won't be finished.

A person must make choices about where they will focus their self-discipline carefully and thoughtfully, using the most logical thinking that they can muster. People may try to eat healthily or work out frequently to have a healthy body, but that does not mean they are inspired to do it. Keep in mind that I am not saying that inspiration and motivation are worthless feelings. I am trying to get across here that the presence of these two feelings can be an unreliable source for somebody to make decisions regarding their life. For some people, inspiration and motivation don't show up until they have already put in quite a bit of work towards their goals. For example, looking to get more muscular might not feel motivated to work out until they got into a regular habit of lifting weights at the gym.

You Might Not Be Doing the Right Things

If you have tried to achieve a goal using various types of angles, but you are constantly failing repeatedly at a certain area of self-discipline, you might have to face the possibility that you have selected something that you simply might not ever be able to engage in regularly. Self-discipline is not only about picking a goal or an activity and doing it despite all costs. Self-discipline is about picking the important activities and goals and doing them against all obstacles. It may be possible that you have simply picked a goal or activity that isn't all that important to you. It is all right to admit that and move forward. The good thing about this is that if it turns out the goal our activity was important to you, after all, it will pop up in your life again thematically, and you would be able to take it up again.

Self-Discipline Fatigue

As we have learned in the earlier chapters of this book, it is extremely tiring and exhausting to consciously fight temptation, select healthy activities, and choose productive activities over unproductive ones. It is tiring because it constantly drains on your willpower resources. It takes lots of energy and effort to turn away from the wrong choices and pick the right ones for your goals. It takes lots of resistance to choose healthy food over unhealthy food that may be quicker and more convenient. It takes a lot of effort to drag yourself out of bed on a rainy morning to get to the gym to work out rather than sleeping an extra hour.

The only way to battle this problem is to practice your required tasks until they become a habit. You want those daily tasks that you need to do to reach a level of automation that you no longer actively think about, and it no longer consumes your willpower resources. Some people may think that all they need is a few weeks or even a few months to build a new habit. This mindset is wrong. Our bad habits are so hard to break because they have been built up through multiple years. Good habits will take the same amount of time. If you have been repeatedly binge-eating whenever you feel upset for the last ten years of your life, except that it will take multiple years before you can break out of that habit and into a healthy eating habit. However, once you do get into that stage, you no longer have to make decisions about that anymore consciously, and they will function on its own.

The good thing is that eventually, with repeated practice and some failures and obstacles along the way, new and better behaviors will become a habit. When this happens, it will consume far less mental resources than it did before. For instance, you probably don't feel stressed out or tired by the idea that you have to brush your teeth at least twice a day. However, if someone asked you to simply workout for 10 minutes a day, which is the same amount of time that brushing your teeth takes, you may find this much harder to do because it isn't already a habit. Like I mentioned before, it just takes a significant amount of time before a new behavior becomes a learned behavior.

Here are some ways that you can address the fatigue that self-discipline may bring:

- There are days where you should incorporate into your schedule to relax and don't have to worry about the things you have to do to reach your goals like dieting or exercising. You can call these 'cheat days' or 'treat days.'
- You can incorporate something called the 80% rule. This means that you accept that you won't be perfect 100% all the time with your tasks or goals, and getting 80% on your goals is acceptable.
- Make sure that you are getting enough rest and sleep. We learned that this is your body's and mind's time to recover from the fatigue we have daily.

CONCLUSION

I hope that through reading this book, you have developed a deeper knowledge of how you can begin to change your life by taking your decisions into your own hands.
I'd also like to congratulate you on having the self-discipline to stick with something and finish this book. You have already proven your ability to have self-discipline; you just need to learn to apply it in other areas of your life. Remember that self-discipline is all about setting goals, breaking them down into smaller ones, and disciplining yourself, so those smaller and daily goals become a part of your everyday routine. When you complete the tasks to achieve your goal becomes a part of your life, you no longer need to draw into your willpower resources to exercise that action. Doing this will leave you more energy to start incorporating other actions of other goals that you would like to achieve. Like I mentioned throughout this book, think of an important goal that you have in mind and work backward and break it down into smaller ones. Start small, and don't give up no matter the obstacles that come your way. I hope that one of the takeaways that you got from this book is that there will always be numerous challenges and obstacles in life.
The key to making any sort of change that will last in your life is consistency. You must be consistent in your practices, change of behaviors, and every component of your new lifestyle to see changes. If, for some reason, you slip up, remind yourself that you are not a failure and continue where you left off. This is how you maintain consistency and make changes in your life.
One important thing that I want to note before ending this off is that everyone has lapses and relapses when changing their beliefs about self-discipline. Like people battling anxiety, depression, or self-esteem, people who are battling with self-discipline may sometimes relapse into their bad habits. This is completely okay. The point here is that you forgive yourself, and you continue practicing the techniques you have practiced this whole time. Just because you have relapsed once, twice, or ten times doesn't mean you have failed. There is no failure here; there is only a forward movement. So if one day you decide to binge-watch your favorite Netflix series rather than working on a paper that's due in a week, that is okay. You may feel bad about it now, but it does not mean you should give up on the process entirely. Simply accept the fact that you had a lapse, figure out what you did wrong at that moment, and apply it to your future growth.
Remember that bad habits take years to build, which means that it will also take years to break down. Rebuilding good habits takes just as long. If you find yourself falling into temptation or you find that it's getting harder and harder to draw from your willpower resources to continue to

do the actions that you promised yourself that you would do, try to think about the purpose behind your goal. Suppose you've learned something from this book, one of the things maybe that a meaningful goal creates more motivation than a goal without substance. Whenever you feel yourself losing motivation or feeling like you're unable to resist temptation, think about what motivates you in the first place to go after that goal. Remember the importance of letting people know you are on a journey of bettering your self-discipline so they can provide you the support and positivity you need to reach your goals.

Lastly, I wish you the best in your self-discipline journey and remember to forgive yourself if you have any lapses on your journey but always remember to keep moving forward.

I wish you luck in your journey, and I hope that you continue to pursue lasting change.

DESCRIPTION

Do you find it hard to exercise self-discipline? Have you ever wanted to change your life, but are unsure of where to begin? Are you tired of always giving in to temptation? Do you have trouble delaying gratification?

Look no further than this book to find all of the answers to these questions and many more. Be enlightened by choosing this book and taking control of your life and habits today.

This book includes the following topics, among others.
- The power of self-discipline
- What is self-discipline?
- The benefits of having self-discipline
- How to delay gratification
- The importance of delaying gratification
- The importance of building better habits in your life
- Good habits that you can build which will help you to improve self-discipline
- The most common causes of having low self-discipline
- How to overcome obstacles in your life by using self-discipline to create motivation for yourself
- How to achieve self-discipline in your own life
- Removing obstacles to discipline yourself
- Utilizing visualization and meditation to help you achieve your goals
- Common challenges of self-discipline that you need to expect
- How to deal with challenges and setbacks in your own life

Self-discipline can be learned and taught; it is not something that you are born with. This is great news, as this means that it is never too late to begin improving upon your level of self-discipline. This book will teach you how to change your life by increasing your self-discipline, which everyone can.

This book not only gives you the information that you need to decide that you need to make a change in your life, but it also contains the solutions that you need to begin doing so. Upon opening this book, you can begin to put these strategies and techniques into practice immediately. This will help you to make lasting changes in several different aspects of your life, including your overall health, your level of happiness, and your relationships, as well as your beliefs and your behaviors. By addressing all of these different aspects of life that make you the person you are, the change will not be in the short term, but it will reach all of the deeper parts of your life.

This book is written to help you understand that treating a problem in your life always identifies the problem. Then, it is important to begin understanding the deeper reasons behind the problem. This book will help you identify the problem, the reasons that you may be struggling with the things you struggle with, and teach you how to deal with this problem and the other problems that come along with it.

By reading this book, you are investing in yourself, your relationships, and your future. Do yourself a favor and decide to change your life by reading this book today! This will help you lead by example and show the people you care about how they can begin to control their lives.

www.ingramcontent.com/pod-product-compliance
Lightning Source LLC
Chambersburg PA
CBHW071407070526
44578CB00002B/506